*In all the world mother nature only knows to pall darkened skies over a house's unknown wonders of lightning chorus white animated synchronized hot flashes spark upon a mountain peak!*

# CHRONICLES
## — OF —
# EMANUEL

*Chronicles of Emanuel: A continuous living hell.*

EMANUEL E. SEWELL

*AuthorHouse™*
*1663 Liberty Drive*
*Bloomington, IN 47403*
*www.authorhouse.com*
*Phone: 833-262-8899*

*Because of the dynamic nature of the Internet, any web addresses or links contained in this book may have changed since publication and may no longer be valid. The views expressed in this work are solely those of the author and do not necessarily reflect the views of the publisher, and the publisher hereby disclaims any responsibility for them.*

*Any people depicted in stock imagery provided by Getty Images are models, and such images are being used for illustrative purposes only. Certain stock imagery © Getty Images.*

*This book is printed on acid-free paper.*

*ISBN: 979-8-8230-1542-4 (sc)*
*ISBN: 979-8-8230-1543-1 (e)*

*Library of Congress Control Number: 2023918580*

*Print information available on the last page.*

*Published by AuthorHouse  11/24/2023*

authorHOUSE®

# ABOUT THE AUTHOR

IT'S THE WINDING TANGLES SEARCHING CHORDS OF WHISTLING ACCORDS OF BLUSTERING WINDS WHICH DO NOT PRETEND; THOUGHT WHEN YOU THOUGHT LOSING LIFE WOULD BE THE END OF STRIFE, A GESTURE OF LOVE BEING ART FIT ME LIKE A GLOVE, AND, ITS MASTER HAS NOT LOOKED LIKE DISASTER. IN THIS MOMENT, THE MEANING OF "THERE SHALL BE NO LOSE" SYMBOLIZES TO ALL THE UPS AND DOWNS THAT SATURATED MY CHILDHOOD WITH ALONENESS AND MANY DISAPPOINTMENTS, FROM SELFISH UNCARING ACTS OF A MOTHER AND FATHER WHO WERE NOT THERE TO NOURISH, MOLD, AND EACH GENUINE TIME I NEEDED TO SHARE SOMETHING WITH EITHER OF THEM THEY SHUT ME OUT COMPLETELY WAS FORCED TO LEARN ON MY OWN...AND I KNOW THERE ARE COUNTLESS MEN AND WOMEN THAT HAVE BEEN DOWN THIS HELLISH ROAD WHERE SUICIDES, ABANDONMENT, ALCOHOL AND DRUG ADDICTIONS MADE "ONE" A SLAVE TO SELF-PITYING!!! IF I ONLY HAD A BRAIN, WHAT WOULD IT PROCLAIM? OH DEAR SIR FLASH BACK WHO'S THAT: INVISIBLE HANDS WITH HUMAN COMMANDS (THEY, SHE AND HE ARE A COMPLEX VARIETY) THAT THIS WORLD NEEDS WHEN YOUR VERY LIFE IS IN SERIOUS JEOPARDY. THE HEAVENS LIT-UP INTO AN EXPANSE ' A SONG AND DANCE' THE FLORAL SHEEN OF OUR HUMAN MEANS. IN THE DAYS OF MY CHILDHOOD SUFFERINGS LEFT WITH MY AUNT "SIS" AKA. ELIZA WILLIAMS ITS THE TIMES WHERE DESPAIR CAPTIVATED ALL MY AWARE, BEING FORCED OUT OF HER HOME TO ONLY GO TO TOMMY THORTON'S FAMILY HOUSE AT 6 AM IN THE MORNING AT 5-7 YEARS OLD WHERE ELSE COULD I GO? HIS MOTHER, ANGIE HIS SISTER, ONE MORE SISTER THEY SHOWED OBVIOUS ANGER THAT I DISTURBED THEIR HOME THAT EARLY. WHAT THEY DIDN'T KNOW WAS THAT OVER THE NIGHT I STRUGGLED GREATLY SLEEPING WITH MY AUNT SIS AND KICKING HER

AND THE MAN WHO WAS HER BOY FRIEND ALL THROUGH THE NIGHT RELEASING MY PAINS, FEARS, THE FACT THAT MY ONLY MOTHER DID NOT LOVE ME!!! THEN, AS THE WEEK PROGRESSED ON INTO FRIDAYS AND SATURDAYS I WAS ON ONE NIGHT SHOCKED BY MY AUNT NOAH (OUR OLDEST LIVING RELATIVE AT OVER 103 YEARS OLD IN 1975 TO 1977), BY THE SCREAMING SOUND WHICH BELLOWED THROUGH ME AS I LOOKED AT HER FACE THEN THIS 4FT. HIGH WOMAN'S PAINS CHILLED MY TINY BONES AND THEN PRICKED MY BRAIN! "THEY KILLED MY HUSBAND, WHO AUNT NOAH COUSIN WILLIAM WILLIAMS SAID? THEN SOMEONE SAID, GET THE BABY HE CANNOT BE HEARING THESE THINGS! COUSIN MERLEE STATED, THEN, BILLY WILLIAMS TOOK ME BY THE ARM AND TOLD TO PLAY OUTSIDE IN THE DARK AFTER 10 PM AT NIGHT. I IMMEDIATELY WENT TO THE WILLIS' HOUSE MY FRIEND BUTTONS (VINCENT WILLIS,) HIS GRANDMOTHER CAME TO DOOR AND SAID, "CHILD WHAT ARE YOU DOING OUT HERE THIS TIME OF NIGHT, I HAD NO ANSWER, SO, SHE SAID BUTTONS IS ASLEEP, SO, MY NEXT OPTION AS SHE CLOSED THE DOOR WAS THE LEWIS RESIDENCE VINSON AND JACQUELINE, MIKE, CLAUDETTE, BIG CURL, BUT MRS. CAROL LEWIS ANSWERED THE DOOR WITH THE SAME RESPONSE, "WHAT ARE DOING OUT HERE? VINCE AND JAQUELINE ARE IN BED. NOW WHAT TO DO I AM 5YEARS OLD ...I AM NOW 6 YEARS OLD ...I AM NOW 7 YEARS OLD WITH THE SAME STORY PLAY BACK AT MY PSYCHE. I GO BACK TO MY AUNTS HOUSE CLIMB THE STAIRS AND FIND A PENNY PUT IT IN MY MOUTH AND STARTED GAGGING AND WOUND-UP POKING SERIOUS LY THAT WAS THE ONLY WAY TO GET BACK IN THE HOUSE CRYING AND HURT.

DURING THE TIMES MY MOTHER (DIANE G. SEWELL NOW WRIGHT ALTHOUGH SHE'S DECEASED), ALL I CAN SAY IS A" LIVING HELL", MEANING, SHE WOULD HAVE SERIOUS TANTRUM'S WHERE ONE TIME SHE SMASHED MY HEAD INTO OUR HIGH-RISE APARTMENT 5-6 YEARS OLD, THEN, TRIED TO COVER IT UP BY DRIVING ME TO THE FIRE STATION AND TOLD THEM A LIE, THAT I WAS RUNNING THROUGH THE HOUSE AND HIT MY HEAD AGAINST THE WALL! OK, BACK TO AUNT SIS'S HOUSE AGAIN, WHILE AT SOME POINT MY MOTHER GOT PREGNANT AGAIN BY GEORGE UNKNOWN, SO, NOW WE LIVING IN DOGWOOD APARTMENTS ROCKVILLE, MARYLAND. IN ADDITION, THE MOST TRAUMATIZING TIME OF MY YOUTH SEE: OUR MOTHER WAS NEVER A CONSISTENT CHRISTIAN SHE KEPT ON "STARTLING THE FENCE" FULL OF HYPOCRISY. THEN AFTER ONLY 1 YEAR SHE FOR THE FIRST TIME LOCKED ME AND MY 1 YEAR OLD BROTHER JW (AKA, BABY GEORGE) IN THE HOUSE FOR OVER A WEEK AND DEMONSTRATED TO ME THAT HER WALKING AROUND NAKED SHOULD HAVE NO AFFECT ON MY PSYCHE? MOREOVER, WHEN SHE KEPT CHANTING THAT DEMONS AND EVIL WAS COMING

FOR US ALL I COULD DO WAS GRAB MY BABY BROTHER AS SHE BEGAN CUTTING HER WRIST WITH A HUGE BUTCHER KNIFE. SHE KEPT TRYING TO CUT HERSELF AS I HEARD THE BLADE WRIPPING ACROSS HER SKIN SHE WOULD JUST SAY, "I CANT EVEN KILL MYSELF RIGHT" THEN, PUKE -UP GREEN LIQUIDS UNKNOWN. THUS, THE KNOCK CAME TO OUR DOOR CHURCH PEOPLE, MY FRANTIC MOTHER WARNING ME NOT TO TOUCH THE DOOR!! SCARED AND STILL HOLDING MY BROTHER WHO PISSY SOAKING WET THROUGH HIS DIAPER, I PUT HIM DOWN AND WITH ONE QUICK DART TO THE DOOR AFTER 10 MINUTES AND UN HOOKED THE CHAIN DEAD BOLT AND THE CHURCH PEOPLE SAVED BOTH OF US FROM WHAT MY HAVE HAPPENED IF WE FELL TO SLEEP? FROM THIS POINT ON FOSTER CARE. THERE WERE SEVERAL MORE ATTEMPTS BY MY MOTHER ONCE RELEASED FROM FIRST FOSTER CARE. SHE TRIED TO BUST MY HEAD OPEN WITH AN IRON, SUBSEQUENTLY, I ESCAPED OUT OF THE HOUSE WITH BARE FEET, EXCEPT FOR SOCKS. PEOPLE CALLED ONE OF HER DOPE DEALING BOY FRIENDS, THEN THE AMBULANCE. MY BROTHER AND I SHIPPED OFF TO FAMILY BRIEFLY AS MY MOTHER PULLED IT TOGETHER BY MARRYING JACK WRIGHT.

WE MOVED TO MY AUNT SIS OLD HOUSE. I WAS ADOPTED BY JACK WHO WAS UNDER COMPLETE CONTROL BY HER. IT WAS THE FACT THAT MY MOTHER REFUSED TO WORK PATHETIC. I HAD SIDE JOBS AFTER SCHOOL CUTTING GRASS ON WEST MONTGOMERY AVE. AND FALLS ROAD ROCKVILLE MARYLAND, AND THE NEIGHBORHOOD NEXT DOOR, THE WADES, AND MS. MABEL AT THE AGE OF 12YEARS WHILE PLAYING BASEBALL IN BETWEEN ALL OF THE MONEY I SAVED AT SIGNET BANK OVER 400.00 DOLLARS, WHILE ALSO PLAYING FOOTBALL FOR RICHARD MONTGOMERY HIGH 1982-1983. WE HAD TO MOVE BECAUSE MY MOTHER WOULD NOT WORK, MY COUSIN BILLY AND HIS GIRL FRIEND LIVED WITH US WITH THEIR DOBERMAN PINCHER "MAX", YET, WE PARTED COMPANY AND MOVED INTO A THREE BEDROOM SUBURBAN APARTMENTS. THE SECOND TIME OF MY LIFE TIME BEING THERE, TONY AND HIS MOM STILL LIVED THERE. HE'S A LIFE LONG FRIEND. I WOUND-UP DOING THINGS THERE THAT NEVER CROSSED MY MIND BEFORE. DRINKING, DRUGS, CHEATING ON MY GIRL FRIENDS, HAVING TO LEAVE SCHOOL TO PAY FOR GROCERIES, CAR.

SO, I LEFT HOME AND AT 16 YEARS OLD ALMOST 17 BY A FEW MONTHS; JOANNE AND I STAYED WITH HER COUSIN SILVIA IN THE SAME TOWN HOUSE WE MOVED FROM TO, MY AUNT SIS HOUSE! I WAS UNABLE TO HANDLE ALL THE PRESSURE FROM LEAVING SCHOOL EARLY BECAUSE WE HAD A BEAUTIFUL BABY GIRL. THE RELATIONSHIP WENT SOUR WHEN JOANNE VOLUNTEERED TO EXCEPT

RESPONSIBILITY FOR ONE OF HER COUSIN CHILD, HELL WE WERE BARELY MAKING IT. I ENDED UP HIRED AT A LUMBER YARD; CINNAMON WOODS RIDE MOWER ASST. FORMAN. FOUND OUT LARRY SMITH, SUPERVISOR WAS MY COUSIN ON MY FATHER SIDE THEN MET MY BIOLOGICAL DAD WHEN I WAS 19 YEARS OLD. HE STILL DID NOT WANT TO BE MY KIN COLD AS ICE BUT THE REST OF THE FAMILY WAS GOOD. MARGIE, LORETTA (LARRY AND PHILLY MOM), ETC. I ENDED UP WRECKING MY TOYOTA CELIC WRAPPED AROUND A TELEPHONE POLE. PRIOR TO THAT, I HAD NERVOUS BREAKDOWN WHERE I WAS ON THE NEWS FOR ATTEMPTED SUICIDE WARING MY VARSITY FOOTBALL JERSEY ABOUT TO JUMP OFF A BRIDGE UNTIL SOMEONE WENT TO GET MY BABY GIRL AND THE VETERAN OFFICER TOLD ME, "LOOK OVER THERE YOUR LITTLE GIRL NEEDS YOU!!!" I BROKE DOWN CRYING AND GOT OFF THE FREE WAY BRIDGE FENCE. I HAD STOPPED TRAFFIC FOR HOURS BLINDED BY DRUGS, THEN HOSPITALIZED FOR OVER A MONTH, BUT WAS ALLOWED TO SPEND TIME WITH MY FAMILY, AND JOANNE'S BROTHER RONALD WEST WAS GOOD PEOPLE AND DROVE ME TO THEM ONCE IT WAS FOUND THAT I COULD NOT TRUST MY WOMAN BECAUSE SHE ALLOWED HER MOTHER TO MANIPULATE HER TOO MUCH.

I BECAME HOMELESS, LIVED BACK HOME WITH MY MOTHER FOR SEVERAL WEEKS THEN MOVED IN WITH JACK ON DAWSON AVE. WHILE I WAS GOING TO COMPUTER SCHOOL IN SILVER SPRING, MARYLAND, GRADUATED, GOT A JOB WITH BOOZ, ALLEN AND HAMILTON AS ACCOUNTING CLERK, THE MAILROOM LOST A PERSON THEY ASK ME TO DO MAILROOM AND FIXED ASSET CLERK DUTIES BETHSEDA, MARYLAND, THEN I STARTED COLLEGE, BEFORE THAT MET JILL AND WE LIVED TOGETHER WITH HER TWO SONS MATTHEW THE OLDEST PLAY ON MY BASEBALL TEAMS OF THE RBBA ASSOC.; LONG STORY SHORT, JILL GOT POSSESSIVE AND INSECURE I MOVED OUT, SHE STOLE MY INHERITANCE WITH THE HOUSE, BOOZ ALLEN MOVED THE COMPANY TO MCCLEAN VIRGINIA, THE COMMUTE TOO MUCH ;STARTED WITH HUGHES NETWORK ELECTRONICS AS ACCOUNT CLERK, STARTED FEELING DESPERATE (COULD NOT COACH ANYMORE WORK COMMUTE, LOSS MY INHERITANCE, LOST TWO WOMEN I THOUGHT WOULD BE THE BEST FOR MY LIFE, AND KILLED MY CHANCES WITH PILLS,ALCOHOL, DRUGS), AND ALL IT DID WAS MAKE ME INSANE!!!

I WOUND-UP BURGLARIZING A MAN, THEN, WAS HELD BEYOND THE 5 YEAR SENTENCE GIVEN LAWFULLY, THE DEPARTMENT OF CORRECTIONS HELD ME ILLEGALLY FOR OVER 23 1/2 YEARS EVEN WHEN THE COURT'S OF SPECIAL APPEALS AND COURT OF APPEALS GRANTED ME "IMMEDIATE RELEASE" FROM THEIR

WRONG DOING; I WOUND-UP BEING ASSAULTED WHILE HANDCUFFED THREE TIMES (FOR FILING CIVIL RIGHTS CASES OF MY INNOCENCE), THEY USED NOLLE PROSEQUE SENTENCES TO "TORTURE POISON, BY FOOD, MEDICATIONS ECT." AND AFTER WINNING MY CASE THE COURT HOUSE OF MONTGOMERY COUNTY MARYLAND BY CHIEF JUDGE JAMES A. BONIFANT, ASSOC. JUDGE CUMMINGS, AND MAGISTRATE SARAH I MALIK; I AM STILL BEING DENIED MY HUMAN, CIVIL, AND TORTURE PROTECTION ACT RIGHTS PROTECTIONS, CIVIL CONTEMPT FROM FAILURES TO FOLLOW YOUR OWN RULES REQUIRE THOROUGH QUESTIONING AND ACTIONS. HOW DO YOU ALLOW A PLAINTIFF TO BE ELECTROCUTED AND SUFFER NECK, SHOULDER, THORACIC, AND LUMBAR INJURIES ON BOTH SIDES IMPINGEMENTS, AND I AM STILL SUFFERING RESIDUAL PAINS. MY CREDENTIALS AS A WRITER FALL INTO THE SPECTRUM SELF PRESERVATION AND LIBERTY AND JUSTICE FOR ALL WHERE LIFE AND PROPERTY GRANTS ALL UNITED STATES CITIZENS THE RIGHT TO FREEDOM OF SPEECH WITH DUE PROCESS OF LAW.

# CONTENTS

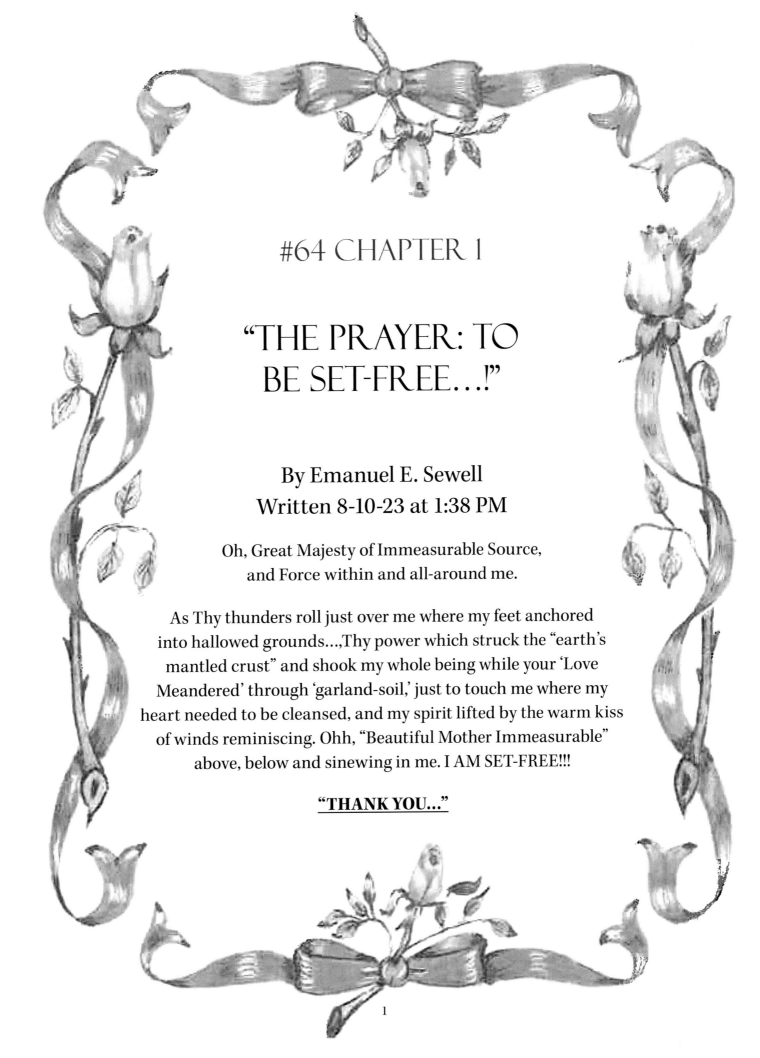

# #64 CHAPTER 1

# "THE PRAYER: TO BE SET-FREE…!"

## By Emanuel E. Sewell
### Written 8-10-23 at 1:38 PM

Oh, Great Majesty of Immeasurable Source,
and Force within and all-around me.

As Thy thunders roll just over me where my feet anchored into hallowed grounds…,Thy power which struck the "earth's mantled crust" and shook my whole being while your 'Love Meandered' through 'garland-soil,' just to touch me where my heart needed to be cleansed, and my spirit lifted by the warm kiss of winds reminiscing. Ohh, "Beautiful Mother Immeasurable" above, below and sinewing in me. I AM SET-FREE!!!

**"THANK YOU…"**

# STEPS INTO THE DEEP…GRANDMA!

### By Emanuel E. Sewell
### Written 10-09-22 to 10-22-22

Dear Grandma, how are you? I sit here and wonder how my life would have turned out were you ever around? Yet, having your DNA in me created an evolving after much suffering and spawns into written prose instead of musical notes or, tap-dancing as you taught my mother. I needed this moment to let you and the world know that there is not any finer time than with your grandmother, she is the "Rock and Soul" of all families second to none a lot of fun to bake cookies with, to help set the tables for Christmas or, traditional giving thanks, and just the times you may be going through tough situations that call for another genuine soul who's life experience can help lead one in the right direction at the most daring and lack of trusting of maturing adult development. So, allow me to share something which has pricked me for quite a long swirling life of karmic challenges. The things I needed from her in childhood upbringing, to know her smile, and to feel her touch by hug, even to watch her sleep peacefully in a rocking chair, so:

"The coastal aqua-marine stunningly in cruise-control seem to clasp-hold of brushing ghostly mist, as the flame of morning time gleams eased with soothing drifts. And though autumn had a spherical wand to tap on emerald-green pressing into earthen realms of scattered leaflets tangerine, yellow-gold, and wet-lit fires of deep red pecking at one's attention just where the "laser-light" glazed even in the lifting overnight haze!

Each calling of the "caped-pall which gave way to ignited day" the buoyant slip-sliding prance an horizon "a-loo-to-a-dance!" Ahhh, it's the orbiting cool brisk wind spinning circuits of arcing embellish, just a nudge of linking wetted slippery trellises inviting each curly-cue of elongated ivy vines interlocking with wooden lattice and beside it swaying to tease at its loosening glance, just a hop-skip-and jump away, the pristine teal mystery of running waters rippling its observing the world over "all aspects should suffice:" 'Purple clovers spright upon the spark of whole moment, and, a josling gift of morning glory with each shoveling and shifting of shade, the inner creeds of sugar and spice flash to the minute just right an imposing delight!" Ahh, don't try to hide your nature prior to empirical adventure.

- **<u>WITHOUT LOVE WHERE COULD WE BE NOW? AS BENT 'MID CLOISTERS DIM' CARESSED BY MOTHER-FASHIONING WHILE EAVES DROP-FALL CAUGHT MY HEARTS' BY SECRETS OF MINISTRY, THOUGH, SHIVERING AT THE MOON…III…CHOOSE…?</u>**

IT'S GRANDMA-HER NAME WITHIN ME THOUGH SHE'S GRANULED TO MY HEART "SWEETER THAN A MOSSY APPLE TREE" NEAR AM I UNTO THEE!!!

AS THE SILENT FIRES IN ME MELTED ICICLES DANGLING IN THE BREEZE…

And as I sat back into green blades of grass my fingers clasped behind my head while looking-up into the crystallite of the days illusionary blue, just for a few seconds rushing passing thoughts of my elder generations perched above and before me, how was it that writing it down became scrolled upon my heart? I instantly became the receiver of the reminded. While I conveyed to stay in touch with each dawning reality, yet, thinking about how life would be if you and I had ever met? So if you're still around somehow this will be my dedication to my "life always to Pauline…"

The tingling chimes hanging off my front porch where a heavy breeze catcher pinging a resonate feeling into my being, how could I not emphasize what I recognized? The dancing silhouettes of shifting-shuffling shadows following each of my heart-beats brought thee (Pauline), closer to me, an aberrant host smooth approach. What one thought you saw sliding-slick into an interior layer of what is woven from an exterior barrier, it is unaccustomed to sufficient sounds ? Yet, a strolling cusp of a whisper on the rebound, I felt us on solid grounds.

Ahhh, criss-crossing the dangling accords like a mighty tidal wave tossing me about, there it was, the rumbling grumble in the trembling annals of time a sweet sound of wind-whistling, where the atoning shivers of human column pillars sought the "burning embers of amaze" which set my soul ablaze! And should the laughter we never had shake the feelings if sad, each timber of cedar oak rooted before me invoke..."Pop-Crackle-Snap" the winding whistle of words crooning off angelic chords chisel the mind of all the ancients of time gone by. The grasping of your absence be it Palpable, Detectable, Delectable, Fantastic, Incredible!!! I found what I'd been missing, the roundabout intangible yet manageable.

- **"THE LOVE OF MY GRANDMOTHER NEVER NEAR, YET, CAUGHT FROM AFAR OFF...WITHOUT LOVE WHERE COULD WE BE NOW? IT'S GRANDMA-HER NAME WITHIN ME...THOUGH III...CHOOSE..."**

It's each provocative jolt and quavering core of my shakened reality sought to chill where the sun-baked sliding glass-pane shrugged-off, how autumn has moved-in, it's the rise and fall of spurning-gale-force swirl, its winds fail-to-pretend. Thus, all of the Greatest of deep-water sources burst the skies-torrential down-pour levy, somehow felt within me! A beckoned saturated tosses of surf's with crashing waves (OH, grandma, where are you now that my suffering be felt by pelting drops...), spiked upon remote protruding gigantic stones, all the ends of the earth casually polka-dotted, to be pounced upon by the sultant-sluice of mighty currents! Oh, heaven, something seems to be a beacon where my burning-souls emptiness is set to boil! Yes, the profound perplexities divine the meaning of moments so unclear where (Pauline) my grandma left me:

- Never felt her kiss upon my eyes, cheek, nor lips...

- Never knew her best attributes, yet, reading, writing, singing, playing the piano or organ, and dance seems to rhythm itself through our generations...

- Never sat at her feet to talk about the things we humans need to relate and navigate...

- Never held her in my arms to console each other's needs...

- Never prayed together to uplift family and each other...

- Never got a chance to look in her eyes, lay my head upon her as heart-beats thumpity...thump...I fall to sleep.

Oh, just like lakes and sandy shores beneath the crags of strong mountain-sides while clouds sip precipitation, a looming solid mural pictured, and, all of a sudden the earth heaved and hoed...Then stood still on its axis while the mantle sickled-hot-lance exploding to burn a flame into my name! The thrust of torched flight sparks spawned mine eyes to the level of gawk where the occasions of my failures and successes were splintered and hovering gossamered to death as silence hunkered in then rang-out,

"Purple clovers ...Purple clovers...Stroke the springing spiked furs of a planted word, and, should the mind-pictured depths of the eidetic viewed in deep-calm to replace the vacancies in my life, thus, my time barrier released, surely "Pauline" took her place beside me.

Thus, the gentle breaths of eternity teach me...Up...Up...Up...So... So...High the 'Apex-of-wonder' thrashed and thrushed its torrents of currents cast off the watery deep and felt me weep!!!

**"STEPS INTO THE DEEP...GRANDMA"**

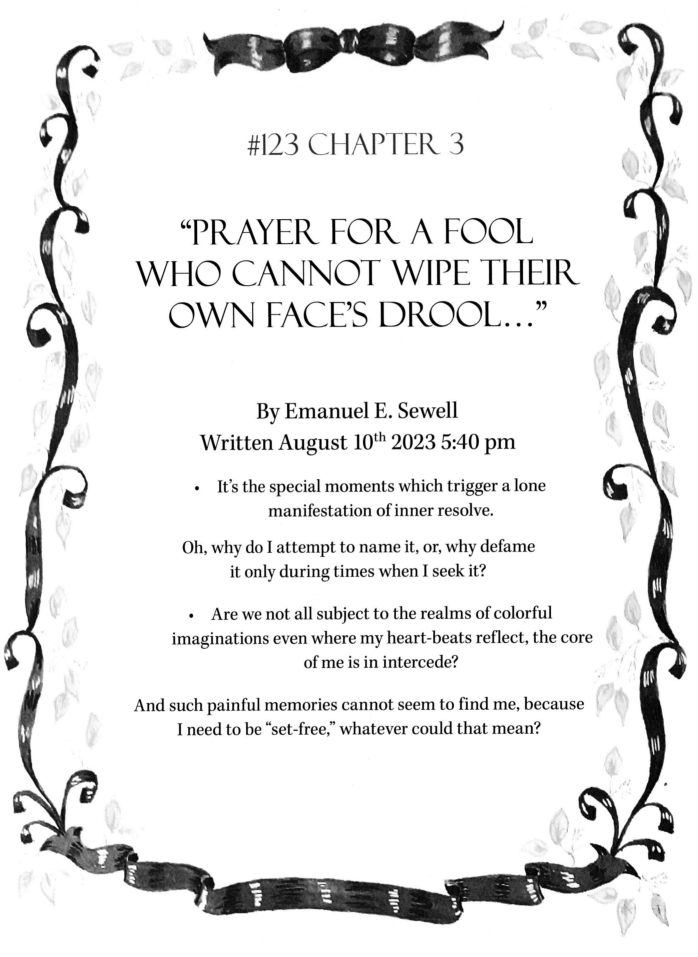

# #123 CHAPTER 3

# "PRAYER FOR A FOOL WHO CANNOT WIPE THEIR OWN FACE'S DROOL…"

By Emanuel E. Sewell
Written August 10th 2023 5:40 pm

- It's the special moments which trigger a lone manifestation of inner resolve.

Oh, why do I attempt to name it, or, why defame it only during times when I seek it?

- Are we not all subject to the realms of colorful imaginations even where my heart-beats reflect, the core of me is in intercede?

And such painful memories cannot seem to find me, because I need to be "set-free," whatever could that mean?

- My lips pressed to my soul sealed by self indecision, delusions, and mine-own confusions only momentarily parted, it is, I, who am a fool thinking that money and power with position must abide in me "all" that I am chasing!

- Yet, as the pedestal of life's experiences just taught me, it's where the imminent domains of power, source and force proclaim its "Anchor," it is, I, again, am he who lost my backbone, my common-sense and my spirituality to ever commune into transforming further developments!

And must I apologize always, and, have I stripped oneself of rational faculties? As I cannot find my inner reality. Such a prayer of this fool, what face am I?

**"PRAY ON INTO WHAT MAY BECOME CERTAIN DEVELOPMENTS!!!"**

# #47 CHAPTER 4

# "GET ON UP…YOU FIX IT GIRRRL!"

## By Emanuel E. Sewell
## Written 6-26-23 to 7-3-23 to 7-10-23

Scene 1 of Contrasted Theme of Macbeth recognized in modern day life whether by symbolic and metaphoric terms the truth is devastating to any living being as you may be annealed by its ending?

Even where the white-sparkle-spright brushed off the moon, where waters tingles-topsy-turvy as the shoreline met each of my foot-steps, they were marred and burnt by some "white, Hispanic, and black-men's fears…" And though 'one man' shows his talents they use envy and insanity, that which cannot be seen it becomes a legion of enemy's…A sinister evil in the hearts and minds of these few blind and empty-souls, who could never properly detect the divine!

"The struggles of innocence and how rulings go abrogated by the unjust prison system hiding their wrongs;

Or, just ignore, yet, you release the ones that are a revolving door! Knowing repeat offenders of gang related violence festers in the halls of Justice, how do you forget the man who helped you continually ?

- Making your sewing shops better by mass production numbers never gained before;

- And multiple skilled in tutoring people with brain tumors and others so illiterate and racist that I had to overlook it because he did not become violent, although his mental illness was reflecting off of what he acted like and visa-versa;

- A library clerk giving all that I had to maintain my sanity where I was to be already home;

- A Editor of the news paper just did not forecast the weather;

- An honorary member of the Sunrise Jaycees-Junior Chamber of Commerce;

- And studied the law so well that I won my case by oneself a total of 5 times, so, why did the DOC interfere every-time? The word accountability seems to have kept them from comprehending that, Ashton v. Brown, 339 Md. 70, 600 A.2d 447 (1995), states,

- "...Plaintiff seeking to establish False Imprisonment need not prove that the defendant's intended to act wrongfully, the essence of the tort consist of Depriving the plaintiff of his Liberty without Lawful Justification, and the good or, evil intention of the defendants does not excuse or create the tort."

- It is clearly no doubt that "COMAR 12.02.06.05 (revised January 1st 2002) granted retroactive "Immediate Release." It took 25 And a half years to become physically free, but, without the Court of Special Appeals Supremacy clause protections of guaranteed rights and remedy! From that point on hell-froze-over the stealing of my mail, the giving my mail to gang related forgers, as death and torture took on a new meaning, what to do? Fight-on-till you cannot go on any longer. The constant food poisoning by Correctional staff controlling the conduct of "state slaves" working in unison also with nursing staff giving wrong medications that have me permanently injured needing major surgeries and unknowns sharp objects planted in my CVS diet, beaten by (11) eleven officers while handcuffed then electrocuted repeatedly where I was not resisting, being kicked in the face until my right eye became trapped in the socket lacerated under it and was punctured eye-ball I bleed profusely, kicked atop my skull so many times that hema-toma blood clot subsided only after 4 to 5 months, then was revealed that my skull was indented to touch the brain, then, forced in the cell I already occupied with a blood gang member went into a coma 5 days in hospital ICU. How the authorities sought to make gangs "king" to replace me from my remedies.

Now back to the poetic tales which fill your imagination with extraordinary wonder:

I am a realized being who dwells not at "hells-gate" as one led astray lost! I must fight through the pangs of pain daily that also at times sends sharp reminders into my brain, as my movements are aligned to nerve damages that will knock you out of any comfort zone even while "gps-beaconed." As what was to provide Heaven became 'sweet waters run dry' Thus, lost its path " sift-slow-sip-swing-low" emotions entangled losing glow, and, no matter that the source seemed to be feminine out running the men?

- **AHH, STROKE THE LEVEL CLOVER PINCH MY MINDS DESIGN NO MATTER HOW LONG I SUFFER, I SHALL NOT GIVEN TO THOSE WHO CREATED MY ENEMY'S."**

- **AND WHERE MY 'SPIRIT SUFFERS' BECAUSE MY CHILDREN ARE NEVER BEFORE ME, HOW CAN I PROTECT, PROVIDE, AND HELP PARENT THEM WHERE HUMANS AS SATAN SEEK TO PULL THE LEVEL FROM UNDER ME ?**

- **OH, I NEED REMARKABLE BENEFITS TO ALLEVIATE ME OF PROMOTING SHAKEN REEDS, WHERE BLOWN-IN GUST GATHER ME INTO ITS TRANQUILITY A TRANSFORMING POWER ONLY FOR ME TO AGREE?**

- **THAT IT'S THE TIME TO REFLECT, RECHARGE, BEING PRODUCTIVE AT THE PINNACLE OF PERCH...AH, ON ONE KNEE I REACH ON...REACH ON... TILL THE BREAK OF DAWN.**

My sonnet to them, "O, wings of a sparrow spread thy comforts to resemble my grandchildren, as the ebb of flowing concentri-circles-concert soothing sounds whistling comparatively to the circuited winds casting forth healing components that invert to caress their hearts...and tap soothe to embrace their young souls strength! All comprehension swivel-swirl-curl toss complexity of our creativity-sensitivity-synchronicity, surprise, we are new inventions, where we have no touch other than invisibility!"

- **<u>GET ON UP...YOU FIX IT GIRRRL...ALL DAY!</u>**

**GET ON UP...YOU FIX IT GIRRRL...SAY IT AGAIN...
GET ON UP...YOU FIX IT GIRRRL...ALL DAAY NEEVER STOP!!!**

(SCENE 2)

## "THE SHIFTING GALES OF GUSTING SAILS, HERE COME MY FRIENDS IN THE WINGS OF CONSORTIUM 'OBSERVING MYSTERY...'"

In the distance of palling darkened skies was 'cast a mirage' of deep dark, crimson haze, and, thus a wheeled –helm spiked all-sparking gleams shone. Yet, a pause as an eclipse-particle-permission a contrast of its lowering drifts, it's when "Heavens Artistry" is fashioned even as friends, who sit at my dinner table...merry in heart...merry in drink (though none alcohol?), still swelling the stomach after all.

So, in the ease of delicate presence sauntered into the midst of bonding developments, where the scent of mirth exercised "vortex swelter" over all-in-every direction as all eyes began to search every person, as if, no-one was present! Thus, where the "bright-dial of reckoning" clutched the corner's of the arching window pane and its laser-lighted gleams leaned on in as if to tell us,(who all were briefly blinded...), what else shall be gleaned from this night?

A brief intermission as the storied life goes: It took a courageous woman (L. Moulden-Wilson) to have me finally removed me from being illegally held without any penological justifications (Civil matters were pending), and against my will after winning the false arrest where an Officer B. Romines, coII kept writing false reports through the States Attorney of Somerset County Maryland. After arriving at Roxbury med. Security, it was back to the same old routine, where I thought things would get better they got very dangerous and worse!

- They just allowed gangs through correction staff to terrorize anyone challenging their wrong-doings;

- They allowed gangs to control picking up Federal Instruments (i.e.; Mailings violating DOC regulations.) giving them the keys to lock boxes in every unit and the keys to the locks that sealed the satchels they carry. Majors, Captains, Lieutenant's, Sergeants, and CoII's all shifts;

- They allowed food service workers to taint the food my body so ravished from it because the crushed pills, rat poison, and unknown substances that had my neck and throat permanently damaged from it by a state slave etc.;

So, to take my mind off it I started writing a proposal for mental health "Life skills Tutoring and Meditation-Stretching and Eating Healthy" over 55 pages then I converted it into four part group sessions with a calendar. So, they stole one idea where I was trying to help people be oriented prior to being released if you had over 5 years served, but, they stole my outline, had inmates given access to my locked locker using a master key, Ofc. Bible and Ofc. Jennings morning and evening shifts I go to eat. They rummaged through my property to provoke me because the SNU staff was trying to extort me when I got funds from my court case through the Governor Larry Hogan, they wanted more.

Then the Asst. Warden threatened me that the compound could get very dangerous if you don't comply. My case manager Tom (We both had worked for Hughes Networks in Germantown MD), so, they trumped-up charges against me (he is delusional all of a sudden) though helped SNU peers get their GED's, then, falsely had me put in isolation cells, then, when I refused to let them take advantage of me they blocked release, blocked me from case after the tier was getting special privileges like: popcorn and movie night, gym time by ourselves, card games then make stir fries with fresh vegetables, ect. Dr. Banks loved the proposal, and Ms. Carrington helped me develop "dual diagnosis' ' through Governor Hogan grants, why did these two people suddenly leave RCI while the infused program was helping the tier? Get rid-of E. Sewell falsely.

### "GET ON UP...YOU FIX IT GIRRL...ALL DAAAY
### GET ON UP...YOU FIX IT GIRRL...SAY IT AGAIN
### GET ON UP...YOU FIX IT GIRRL...NEEEVER STOP!"

**And just when the night crawled ...**a cooling gale blew soft over my feet, it's as if we-all were "stung still." Where a kindling took hold and shifted 'the fire-bug' to consume any human hesitation! Ahhh, what is this? The matrix of wonder crossed over all seasonal mixture, it's just an 'enchanted garden' that brought forth a whisper of an "empirical tale" which pricked the ear and stilled all the world to listen!

Oh, that we in-part were chilled, rattled, anew yet are fortunate to hold the "Golden Chalice", a tender moment to sip honey-suckle mixed with rain...As in one motion the cup sought to leave my hand? And even as no elixir had clouded this event, because the bottom rung was empty of its "Royal Gems" that had traveled the world over.

Thus, we rose from the table as "one" with not a word spoken, not even a flinch, and not a glimpse into the other's eyes, stunned! Then, in 'one-fell-swoop' the distance from the moon beckoned our calls into silence, to awaken and hinge our Love to Forever, as a decree, to crush with the sledge-hammers of law and humanity the "burning embers of change" dowse all evil-doers even as death itself is the "All-knower."

**<u>"GET ON UP…YOU FIX IT GIRRL…ALL DAAAY<br>GET ON UP…YOU FIX IT GIRRL…SAY IT AGAIN<br>GET ON UP…YOU FIX IT GIRRL…NEEEVER STOP!"</u>**

(Scene 3)

**"Just as the petering shadows crossed-over the squint of golden-crystal-spiked-dunes, yet, the night had already set-in, how could its drift be viewed?"**

Here she comes, if the earth had no rotation we as human beings would be without "copulations!" It is the "Woman" who refines the mind of all mankind, and, without Her-mother-earth-functions "We would All Be Nothing!" All shadows can be cut-in-twain by a meridian plain horizontal domain, to never-ever return to "us" the same. The-world-over in sweet pleasant concrete beyond granite stills the ground beneath my feet.

Just a step further, sure am I to never sleep while 'weeping-willows-creep' for in the loss of my step,(From a long day's work…), it only lies to close my watery eyes. I suppose the earth circling on its axis receives the clusters of starburst universally usurps its center to "set-fires-ablaze" and clear morning haze. So, step to the quick light of my life with sweet glaze dripping over wafting-marmalade. This is to all the Queens of the Earth you are bequeathed this serenade!

What dwells deep and perhaps dormant there will always be a "determinate…" As we can tell though man or woman sitteth upon a citadel. No winking eyes, a desire drowned by the "Inner-Candles-Yearn," so, when the path is cleared it reveals no fears. And once thy "Aura-Spright" shaking mist with the shade coming into form easing out of the green glades, It Is the Woman who issues forth life, and, not to be exchanged for the deranged!

(Scene 4)

Where the annals of time traversed its influential deposit of 'subliminal-phase,' deep-space-static it's incomprehensible though self-relied on from previous lives, (Just memories of forgotten experiences), thus, decades gone by incrementally inspired. There will be no dramatic speculations with gossamered transposition to mold the things to come making no conclusions into the vastness of what permeates

"Beautiful Immeasurable;" A gripping impetus of sensitivity star-gazing-sizzles the seams of muonic streams helix-polarity caught chromosomes (y/x) concentric-tickle-me "think" projecting 'Life-Long' realities…

"Oh, trickled waters once sweet running over my bare- feet eased on into embedded stones, shall the mountain wonder, where the evident marvels of the universe has always blinded mankind's vision to those elements escaping attention?"

What pray-tell is this?

- The binary and radicals relationship: 1). Arithmetic using two's (2) as its base;

- 2). A binary code system which "kissed the hulk" of all computer missions O"s and 1's anyone;

- 3). And even in the binary-star-system two clusters as "wholes" orbiting together;

- 4). How did "All-Humanity" fall off the binary tree? Where the record shows, "the branch to the left structural data shows greater than the right, then, lesser its opposite- binate growing in parts (What human beings can be justified as being divided of oneself while growing!) Just to clear the confusion;

5). Thus, comes the radical compounds "Atoms" which "remain unaltered" during any ordinary chemical or biological changes! (Emphasis Added By Oxford Dictionary-Scholars);

**"GET ON UP...YOU FIX IT GIRRL...ALL DAAAY...
GET ON UP...YOU FIX IT GIRRL...SAY IT AGAIN
GET ON UP...YOU FIX IT GIRRL...NEEEVER STOP!"**

Then, passed the baton in its orbital traisp to (Webster's New World College Dictionary) Provided the real-deal: A. Binary being composed of two elements/radicals of (1) one; Now, to binary fission is asexual reproduction, meaning, "By spitting of a cell into equal parts..."

Who of you have re-entered the womb, Whom of you can make happen what nature has not invested in you?

Because Atoms (are radicals), for which we are all inescapably fashioned "single-Atom," and, goes through a reaction "unchanged," or, is replaced by a "single-Atom" it is "INCAPABLE OF SEPARATE EXISTENCE." Oh, chill my contracting grip we have got to fly-higher and resonate with the new view that has come into our "Human Relationships!" And, spiked-spangled-plumes caress the furs of a planted-word. All my "Divine" bloom from the' Sun-lights-Kiss...' Oh, still-my-soul maceration haversacked into ovulations will always dominate "My Generations!"

**"GET ON UP...YOU FIX IT GIRRRL...ALL DAAAY!"**

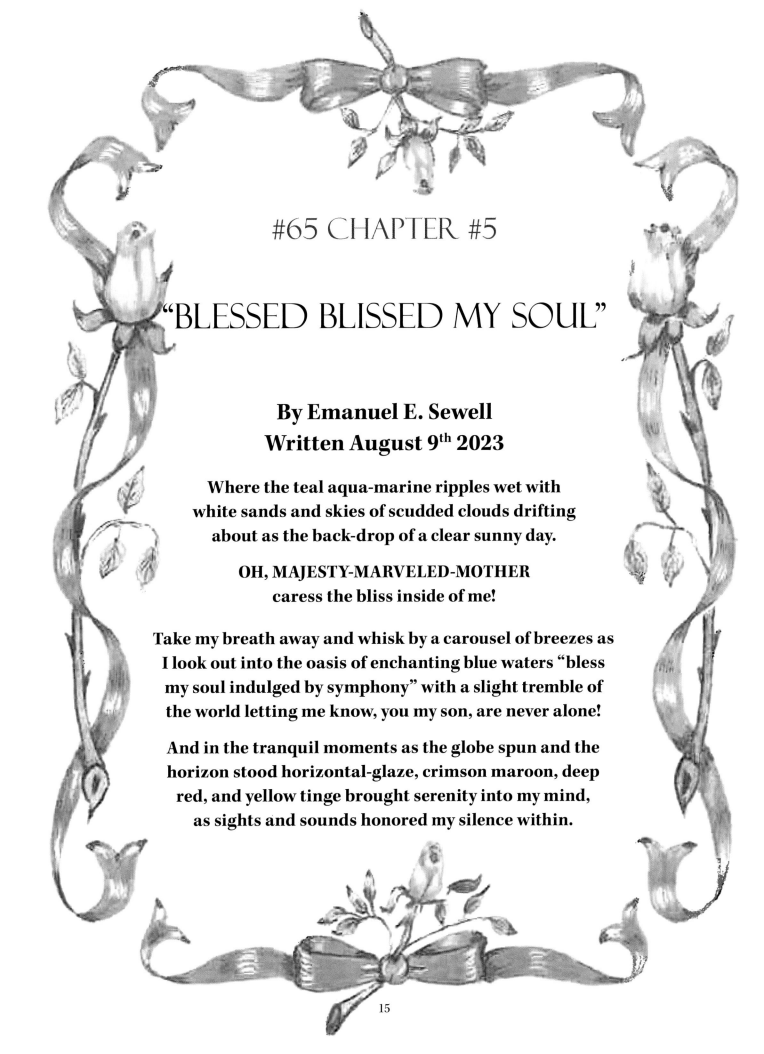

# #65 CHAPTER #5

## "BLESSED BLISSED MY SOUL"

**By Emanuel E. Sewell**
**Written August 9th 2023**

Where the teal aqua-marine ripples wet with
white sands and skies of scudded clouds drifting
about as the back-drop of a clear sunny day.

OH, MAJESTY-MARVELED-MOTHER
caress the bliss inside of me!

Take my breath away and whisk by a carousel of breezes as
I look out into the oasis of enchanting blue waters "bless
my soul indulged by symphony" with a slight tremble of
the world letting me know, you my son, are never alone!

And in the tranquil moments as the globe spun and the
horizon stood horizontal-glaze, crimson maroon, deep
red, and yellow tinge brought serenity into my mind,
as sights and sounds honored my silence within.

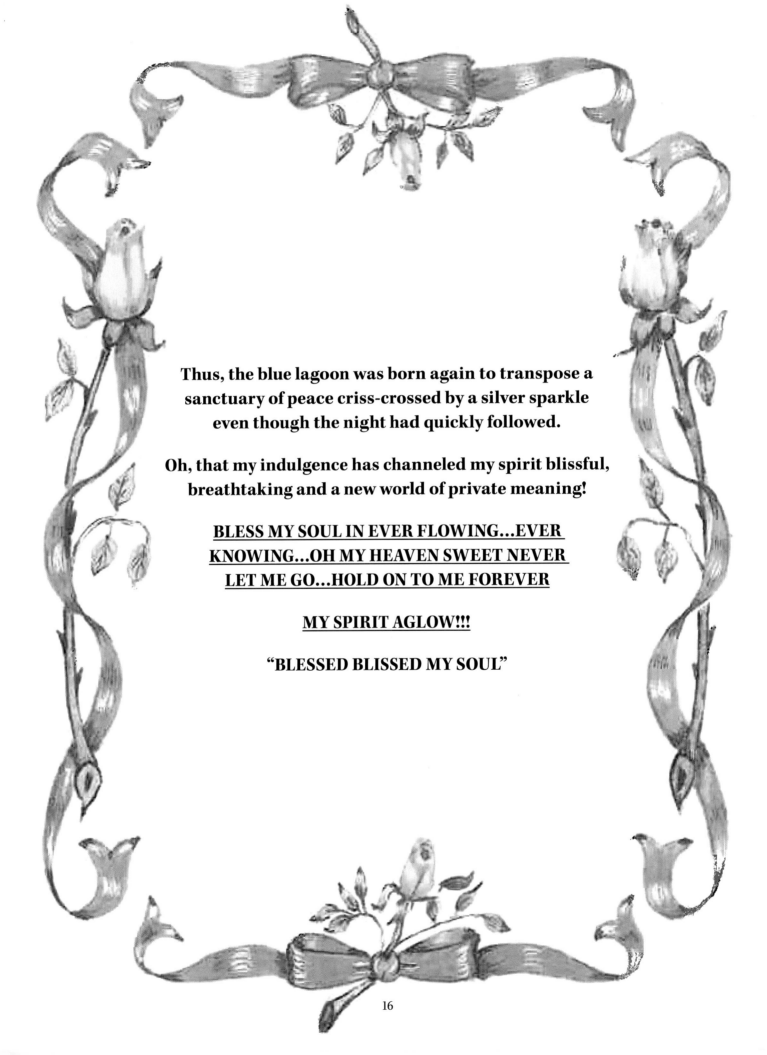

Thus, the blue lagoon was born again to transpose a sanctuary of peace criss-crossed by a silver sparkle even though the night had quickly followed.

Oh, that my indulgence has channeled my spirit blissful, breathtaking and a new world of private meaning!

BLESS MY SOUL IN EVER FLOWING…EVER KNOWING…OH MY HEAVEN SWEET NEVER LET ME GO…HOLD ON TO ME FOREVER

MY SPIRIT AGLOW!!!

"BLESSED BLISSED MY SOUL"

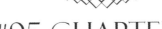

# #95 CHAPTER 6

# "DRIFTING OUT OF DARKNESS INTO THE LIGHT RECEIVE ME... 'THOUGH I CHOOSE...!"

## By Emanuel E. Sewell
## Written as Part Two 4-10-22

A frosty-dew to a brand-new start the misty sheen of what does adore
you mean? It's a turning point if you must 'ashes to ashes and dust
to dust' brush oneself off in the gradual changes into conversion
woven as the wombs of "sister soul train" in its grooves!

Ahhh...my affections are not of pleasure, they ride the gale
with force which helps me to make mine own choice.

So, tickle me tender, fickle me blue, and bound around 'cut-to-the-chase' to kiss my lips
only from a woman's taste can my heart-beats drift cyclic-cycle me embraced by you!

Rumble...Young Soul Man...Rumble these be the times again
you must ride with the sail in a mettle lifted by all four cornered
winds, The power of love for us to begin again and again!

Drifting into darkness...an authenticity linked by brevity into the myths of
mystery caress my adulation out of hesitations performing symphonic...pass
the baton surreal tamped-down, and then, brought up by the "real deal,"

Our lives have come to pass clashed-jejuned fragmented light lament echoing simmered-sooth, the soul drifting uneased while the impetus of love sipping my glow I thought I'd lose control being taken within my-own body "OH GREAT BEING" rarify my soul, again, I thought that life meant for our essences to intertwine, could "You" really be mine? The compassionate connection a worthy development from all my troubles...

Though I choose...?

Well...Well...Well...I was drifting into darkness...Oh when my mother died I had no place to hide even where my life had already been vindicated by the Appeals Courts of Maryland on both-sides, yet, still being held innocent as a "slave of the state" (being beaten and killed more times than humanly imaginable fighting still for my freedoms!) taking over 25 and a half years of my life from me, my daughter, and my three grandchildren, how many more tears, how many more years?

**"SHALL I LOOK ABOVE...TO LAUGH AT THE MOOON...
AS MY MIND BE ON THE CHIII...!**

**"A SERENE MIND IN ME WITH THE GOOD AND PLENTY, SO SWEET INTO YOU, IT'S WHY MY ACHING HEART CAREENS BLUE AND THE RIBBON FLAILS ANEW, IT WOULD BE A BONNET SINGING-OUT MELODIC-SONNETS..."**

**'A MISTY SHEEN OF WHAT DOES ADORE YOU MEAN?'**

Let the years of searing undried tears bearing the untold become stolid in the heart so bold! It was caressed by a sheen screen of misty haze adrift of what caught my sight with tiring eyes an adoring sift as in my leaning around a stony labyrinth: There have been no drugs and alcohol apart of my life in over 20 plus years, those were the times of "drifting into darkness...I couldn't find my way and had no other family who cared or, knew to care!"

I've always been on my own from the ripe age of 5 years old to right now at 53 years young (The sporadic changes from foster care back to unstable parent constantly...), thrown into drifting darkness...to fend for oneself...Now makes my mind be on the chiii...! Ah, my LOVE above and between us being gravity who bequeath the seams of true inner means, is it all I need? The compassionate connection is a worthy development from all my troubles...Though I choose...?

Well...Well...Well...I was drifting into darkness...All my troubles I did not choose...Abandonment had no rules, a mother and father with no heart, where could a child possibly start? Even in the rain coming down as the sprinkles from heaven as a child I walked alone up and down the streets of the ghettos no matter how far the expance of my life is where you are, and, the helm realm from above spread-out dynamic where oscillating prisms meet each rainbow eidetic-metric-selected-electric-imbued, Fantastic!

Flash back...when I heard my mother say, "get out, get out of the car startling me then my brother cries at one year old along with me so many times she tricked us." While my cousins never knew when we were ever going to 'surprise' them; Being left to no nurturing or safety, no genuine care or concern, no food, my cousins hating me-too many mouths to feed, and at times no shelter for me only as everyone was struggling!!!

**SHALL I LOOK ABOVE...TO LAUGH AT THE MOOON...
AS MY MIIIND BE ON THE CHIII...!**

**<u>"OH THAT MY MIND REHEARSALS SOFT APPROVE INTO THE EVENINGS MOODS AND WHERE THE MOONS SILVER SPARKLE CUT THROUGH THE TOWNHOMES SIDEWALKS TO LIGHT MY SHOES, ONCE AGAIN, JUST TO YOU WHEN I OPEN MY DREARY EYES TO SEE MY ONLY FRIEND INVISIBLE WITHIN TENDER MOMENTS OF LOVE ON THE WAY THOUGH PALLING CLOUDS HAD NO MORNING KISS OF ITS SUNS GLAZE, WOULD THIS NIGHT CREATE NEW DAYS UPON THE WINGS OF ANGELS JUST BENEATH MY SKIN?"</u>**

**'A MISTY SHEEN OF WHAT DOES ADORE YOU MEAN!'**

A cherry blossom within two hearts' (of my mind and what pumps red-golddd...), absent branches no chance for happenstances and that which shielded our spirits blended into the cove, and at first glance the hawk arose, thus, the swelter of my breath penetrated true missions and within the octave of my chants came pure tastes, a garden of inner transformations once thought to be a 'spiritual coffin' became the bended knees of quiet sensitivity!

Now, alive clutched in the mind just a little too much without my caressing touch, its quiver-quiet-quick shivers have a start in me before it's too late Up...Up...Up my spirit awakes when they took my life away...drifting into darkness take my miiind beyond the chiii...Take my miiind beyond the chiii! I could not even call to my father (As I was told he's Robert though he was Howard, then adopted he's Jack.) Could I search for more as my eyes clamped to the skies nocturnal blue, all of me lied to, is what transcends into all of yooou. And never met my big brother, grandmother, aunts, uncles, and cousins until I was raising my own family at the ripe age of 19 going on 20 years old. I was unknowingly drifting into darkness...left my girl and my 2 year old baby girl after a car accident hitting a telephone pole and careened into a gas station and was taken to the hospital, now, my life had no claim to fame! The compassionate connection is a worthy development from all my troubles...Though I choose...?

Well...Well...Well...I was drifting into darkness...All my troubles I did not choose... The WAR of my mother's mind, confusion and selfishness was my outcry into the great blue skies...Ah, where is my savior? Wooo...Hooo...wooo...drifting into darkness pretty soon, how would I pay? As working in Corporate America (Booz*Allen &Hamilton Consultants and Hughes Networks Virginia and Germantown) all those years of free college just keep a B average, then, Surprise! No more Coaching Baseball 1 year from potential Championship my job moves to McClean; My second fiance' I lose my first home to greed and aversion by a woman, who could only hear her own voice now she lives alone not by choice, how I lost my choice while falsely incarcerated (from a corrupt system using "nolle proseque charges"), cut off my voice!

**(THE DOOBIE BROTHERS, said it best, "Without Love Where Would You Be Right Now?")**

**<u>RISE...RISE...RISE...WERE IT NOT FOR THE LOVE ABOVE AND WITHIN US MY REMEMBRANCE WOULD BE 'DROWNED IN EMPTY RIVERS,' THUS, SAVED ME BEFORE THE SACRED BREATH AND ITS HORIZONTAL GLOW AT THE EDGE OF WHAT WE-ALL HAVE COME TO KNOW!</u>**

**"A MISTY SHEEN OF WHAT DOES ADORE YOU MEAN..."**

**<u>DRIFTING OUT OF DARKNESS INTO THE LIGHT RECEIVE ME...THOUGH I CHOOSE...!</u>**

# #69 CHAPTER 7

# "TO NEVER BE FAR APART AND THE SMILE THAT YOU SEND OUT 'RETURNS TO YOU IF YOU ONLY HAVE A HEART"

## By Emanuel E. Sewell

### "DEDICATED TO: CALEB, ALANA, AND MICHAEL"

The smile that you send out returns to you to stay bright, young,
and chipper, so, don't forget to lock it with a zipper!

ALANA AND MICHAEL ASK : OOOh, granddad,
how could you do that 'SILLY WILLY?'

Well if you-all were not so far apart there would be no need to have
Caleb build a "go-cart" perhaps we'll get a headstart?

CALEB ASKS: Oh, where do I go to get the parts, I will need a turbo and a supercharger!

When opportunity seems flimsy I follow the wisdom 'aroma-
atmospheric' (Just the places you know that have auto mechanics.)
And to fill-me-in where I may be missing, if I only had a heart?

To behave in such a way my inactions seem to fill my days, just to 'coin a
phrase' and fill my mind with better days instead of an empty kettle!

Let my limbs sprout about brand new with mettle.
And no longer separate or far...apart.

A chorus of glee went out by Caleb, Alana, and Michael…Yeahhh!
Granddad is to be close and we have conquered being far apart.

And if only I'm resumin' a picture-fade cartoonist,
how could you decipher my movements?

Could I ever be a puppet? So that you fill me with vocabulary and parts of
speech like, syllables, prefixes, even a suffix is common amongst us…

So, translating a humorous contemplation, I, "dub thee" a spelling bee…Caleb
says,"And now I feel human coming alive for all to see!!! Alana, "wow could that
really be?" Michael, "I'm just here to have fun with my Poppa Hano, has it begun?"

**IF ONLY I HAD A HEART
INSTEAD OF GIBBERISH
I COULD EXPRESS WORDS
AND NOT BE PUT IN A PETRI DISH
I WOULD BE PRICKED,
I WOLUD BE MOIST AND SO FULL OF CHOICE!
SUCH REGARDING LOVE, KINDNESS, AND THE BEAUTY
OF ART ALL-AROUND AND ABOVE US…**

**And why not be friends with "all" that nature extends?**

**Thus, we-all are healthy with raspberry, cherry, and even blue-
berry which love's to be eaten covered in cream with cinnamon
oats, just where my tummy and taste-buds like it most!**

**Caleb, Alana, & Michael chime, "You are making us hungry,
let's go to the kitchen and make something yummy."**

**Just one moment while I'll figure it out if I only had common-sense to grant me
one wish? Michael and Alana jump in, "I wish for a big ol' plate of fruity berries
and cherries in yogurt and I wish for waffles and cream with juice granddad!"**

**Before that just watch a gentle peach, white, and dotted flowers unfold
while misty-brushed-wet within the hour comforting us with peace, love,
and joy supreme, a higher reach within to cherish being friends.**

Oh, how beautiful the smiles I see with laughter and full of ready to eat! Well, let's set-up nap time "SESAME STREET" just before we eat, so, where are your clean white sheets as nap-time may tug at me after all the tasty food we eat; OH, granddad I can finally hear your heart-beats as I lay my head on your shoulder and chest, Alana and Michael attest, where are your's? Since I am the story-teller I must know before we retreat, how sweet, I just heard the first beat and the second, what about you Caleb are your beats in rhythm too, listen, ahh.. that's good to review.

And all your smile's are giddy as we prepare our meal for this wonderful day and just to measure my emotions to calm my heart with sweet aroma! It seems that devotion is absolutely the right start that will keep us from being;

"TO NEVER BE FAR APART AS THE SMILE THAT YOU SEND OUT RETURNS TO YOU IF YOU ONLY HAVE A HEART."

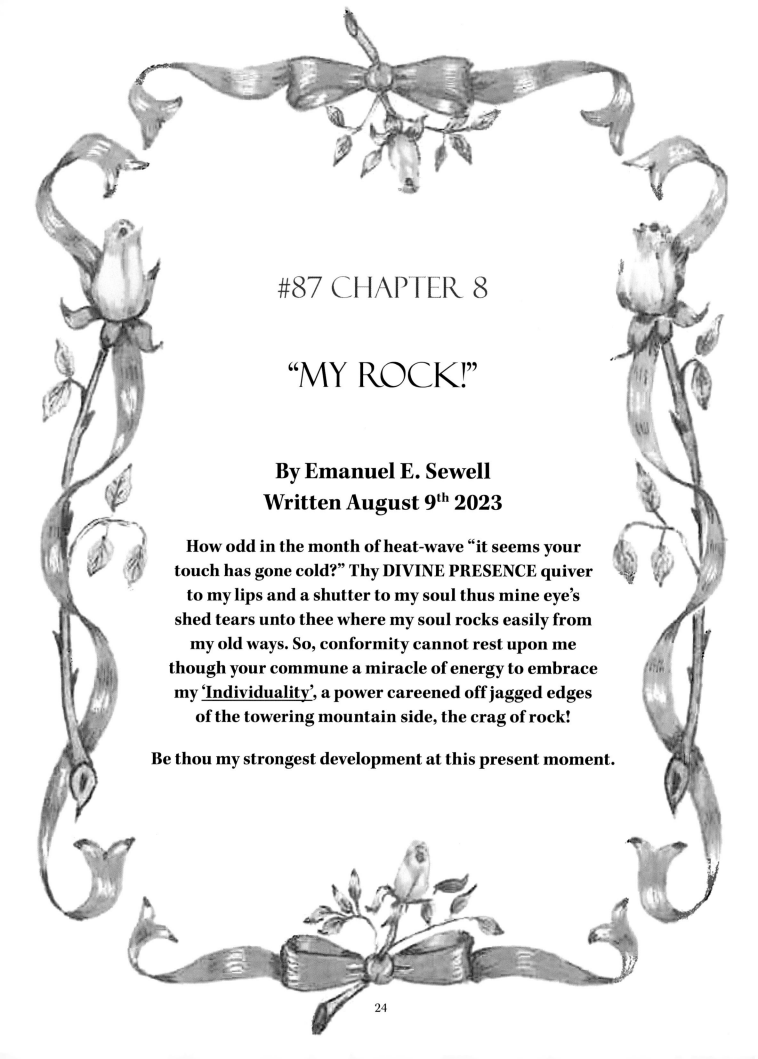

#87 CHAPTER 8

## "MY ROCK!"

**By Emanuel E. Sewell**
**Written August 9th 2023**

How odd in the month of heat-wave "it seems your touch has gone cold?" Thy **DIVINE PRESENCE** quiver to my lips and a shutter to my soul thus mine eye's shed tears unto thee where my soul rocks easily from my old ways. So, conformity cannot rest upon me though your commune a miracle of energy to embrace my 'Individuality', a power careened off jagged edges of the towering mountain side, the crag of rock!

Be thou my strongest development at this present moment.

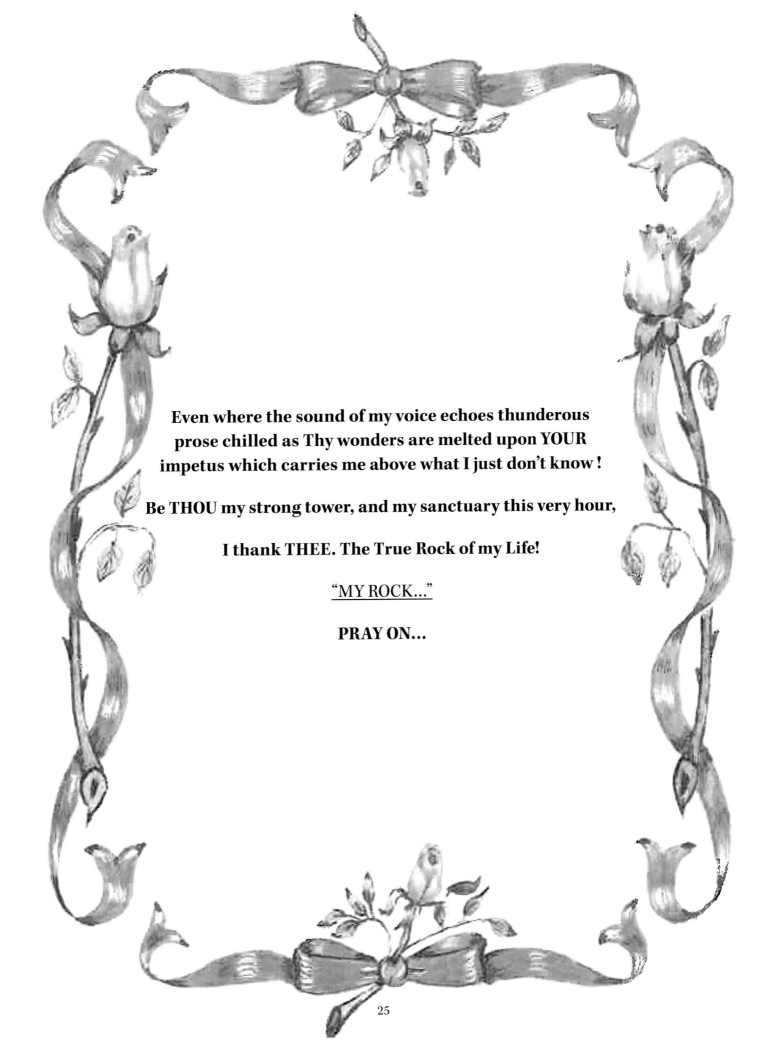

Even where the sound of my voice echoes thunderous
prose chilled as Thy wonders are melted upon YOUR
impetus which carries me above what I just don't know !

Be THOU my strong tower, and my sanctuary this very hour,

I thank THEE. The True Rock of my Life!

"MY ROCK…"

PRAY ON…

# #99 CHAPTER 9

# "FLASHBACK…WHO'S THAT?"

## By Emanuel E. Sewell
## Written 4-23-22 to 5-1-22

The Morning came into being so discrete simple over seemingly pleasant coalescing motivated "swing-sweet-low," casting helms from above to sprout forth my wings as a dove chasing darting swills while the humans below sat on park benches with a radio listening to melodies. But not knowing their conversations? They were visited by some woman who kissed one gentleman, saying,

"Let thy innocence spike an accord sacred to those who share my same blood."

As gentle breezes croon a 'cool subtle mood' while we peered into partly clear and cloudy sky ripple-skittering fluffed-scudded-puffed like white cotton in its search for a patch of earth…Plush be the heavens my high gorgeous calm harmonize me serene with 'every walk of life' most notable those peaceful and meaningful amongst "us" and let not any crackling banter disturb the amazing.

"All thy vastness of heavens powers stroke the level clover and penetrate me with 'LOVE' within too course the life I live without avarice!"

Though temptations swirl about mixed in with feral winds, but, it's the beacon of a moments treasure which keeps us together.

It is the lives of friends that send sweetened aroma to assert life to begin… Jasmine a satisfaction of our attraction, and listen, it's the 'song birds' setting us at ease (Pray tell it must be meeee!) soaring about helping the blossom's of fig and fruit trees.In setting a course for my life:

**Flashback Who's That?** Destined to punctuate 'Des pre' (French for "a man of wit"), in my heart-beats haste it varies with taste, oh, that my tongue split not its purpose! Never to slander, never to deny a good deed, never to swear, and never to not care.

To honor the sequence of lives-lived self-glow, a grace indeed, even a slip-cover for one's in need...don't make it hard for me, rain again? How interesting 'apple jack's' sift the honeysuckle-sweets just a treacle of what we need in the cross-over exchange of the greet and meet. And don't sugarcoat your mood 'skip-to-maloo' one heart beat times two equals me and you!"

## "NO MORE FARE-THEE-WELL WE ARE LAUNCHED SO EXCITED REAL CLOSE COMING BACK TO YOU!"

**"FLASHBACK WHO'S THAT?:** Candy-rain dewing-down touched on in easy upon casted gleams falling into a custard cream dream with twisted cinnamon wetted petals of the rose of "SHARON", all humanity back down memory lane 'smiling faces going places being happy with good cheer!' Have you got happy feet again because there's no time for hate so matriculate, the feeling and healing of love hold me, caress me as our "Beauty" seems to say we are "One" in the glow of "Love!"

**"FLASHBACK WHO'S THAT?:** The nature all-around dancing to"the ski-above ablaze" my tears seep while my heart weeps into the rotations of the Heavens lit-up 'a song and dance' our hearts and minds with right actions designed even as the "azure skyline took flight" all our human means collected into the capering whirlwinds as we begin! There a sparkle before the night caressed the mind of all mankind satisfied... Too feel real happiness...To feel our pains subside...And the way you hold me no-way LOVE could die...imbued-eclectic-electric-semetric-enigmatic-fantastic!!!!"

**"FLASHBACK WHO'S THAT?:** Bitter-sweet calling on 'back down memory lane,' can you save me? Summoning once again "candy-rain" in your name and wetting my eyes there's no disguise, the Heavens talk, my mind walks, as my hearts skips into new views we can no longer be considered "fools" where our rarified souls are renewed!"

**"FLASHBACK WHO'S THAT?:** The motivated beauty of the day extend white fiery claps that command "The changing directions of our lives" from the days, months, and years of dreary-weary-confusion bemoaned now 'Bear-Hugged' like the column stalk of an aged sequoia, "Smacked...Sizzled...Chiseled...Charred...Smoked," its sap weeped and seeped with the tears of an invoke hunkered in too sweet just right as it split the memory of family branches in 'Threes fiery bright' so...so...good! Now take this moment of ours into your hands upon the "Beautiful Immeasurables'" Demands!!!

## **"NO MORE FARE-THEE-WELL WE ARE LAUNCHED SO EXCITED REAL CLOSE COMING BACK TO OUR INNATE-NATURAL VIEWS!"**

## **"FLASHBACK WHO'S THAT..."**

# #94 CHAPTER 10

# THE ALONE TONIGHT…

## BY Emanuel E. Sewell
### Written 10-11-21 to 9-11-22

### "UNIVERSAL DECLARATION OF HUMAN RIGHTS"

Now, therefore, the General Assembly proclaims this Universal Declaration of Human Rights as a common standard of achievement for "all peoples and all nations." To the end that every individual and every organ of society, keeping this declaration constantly in mind, shall strive by teaching and education to promote respect for these rights and freedoms and by progressive measures, national and international to secure their universal and effective recognition and observance, both among the peoples of Member States themselves and among the peoples of territories under their jurisdiction.

And to take a moment of quiet reflection emptying oneself in silence while we still go through inhumane practices I shall render my hearts' to what is "Beyond Measure…":

### #61 TAKE MY HEARTS'-SHOW ME HOW SWEET LOVE IS?

"In the dawning of sophisticated croons, oh, Thy maestros of discipline, appreciation, and when it's time to strum-the-chords out of secreted fjord's, just seep-out wisdom! As YOU stand firm upon the plateau's and to reach underneath where rare velvet and white striped with ribbon blue orchids are so protected in the crag of granite-stones which send chills into my very bones! Oh, 'MOTHER-NATURE' my refined grace make haste to grant me the days of power, love, mercy, and equality as a boost of creativity, a quality of living, and the meditative abilities to conquer stress, evil intentions, and heightened cognitive sensitivity, and that, in these trials brevity "Royal" my days above-the-dens of my body impingements!!!

**"TAKE MY HEARTS'-SHOW ME, HOW SWEET LOVE IS!"**

THANK YOU...PRAYER UNTO 'YOU.'

Thank you for empathicly listening to some of the most vital aspects of our lives that are crucial to our progressing as a humanity that its conscience be pricked while unlawfulness becomes more prevalent violating our existence as a people, and you will be reminded how critical this sharing is for congress and senate to make the same strides we have made as if it were still 1948 when the United Nations General Assembly "ADOPTED..." And by the aforementioned introduction, and those Articles of incorporation herein after.

It seems very trying living alone as the nights and days marshal away, yet, my spirit gets stronger when I keep loved-ones memory alive within so the story is one where sadness envelops me at times being human, then, moments of exhilaration because of the major survival after all these painful years, is there finally a meaningful measure of my daily transformations?

"Where the pitch-black azure-skyline marshaled in billowous clouds surrounding its calling-cards which helped the sun split the vastness of a watery surface churning the invisible-sublime! Even as the earth's waters touched-over-easy by a casted rays parting upon each encroach of sandy crystallite cooled in its glisten, to still all the earth to listen!

'It was by rotating command that the sun called on crimson to remove 'particle-permissions (Its Hands), by my parochial demands!'

All these many years (27 years of major difficulty)

It seems self-indulgence allowed me to clearly see

Oneself for the first time, though non-judgmental of who I am and what I have become, there's never any conflict with right from wrong, so, why was I chosen to suffer so much early...in between...and now?

- I have sacrificed as a young professional, father;

- Life time volunteer for my Rockville MD communities, and;

- An honorary member of the chamber of commerce etc

- Frederick MD Literacy Council Certified Tutor etc.

I made decisions so young that people were shocked that I owned a home at the age of 23 years old. So, why did my own mother disown me because I was engaged to marry a Caucasian woman, yet, allowed our cousin to live with us with his girl the same the craziest things; her mother taught her how to survive by teaching her to play piano, tap-dance, read and write by my grandmother but so pathetic refused to even care when we were constantly moving where her excuses failed us every-time no energy or capacity to care for anyone except self, (And my brother just like her "man you gotta let the past go...after saving his life so many times as a child!) Such a fool to allow the past to kill you in silence. No soul can attain liberation without traveling into what brought you to this point, then, reconciling can come about, who suffers to fester in trauma by never addressing what got you there? Only a fool who fails to wipe his face from his own drool, how could one ever attain victory wallowing in pain, psychological, psyche, and the visible scarring which he has plenty as a reminder. My life is so much more richer (No more drugs, alcohol, self-pitty, depressions that make you want to kill yourself because you watched your mother do it time... after time...), even in my spirit and soul where I faced the demons during which 11 racist Officers beat me handcuffed into comas had I not delt with it I'd be "silly-puddy" ineffective to oneself and society, yet, this very minute...this very hour...this very time that has past molded me and fashioned my efforts to blossom and flower like never before though I am still being denied my Supremacy Clause Constitutional Rights Guaranteed! :

- Article #21, says, "Everyone has the right to take part in the government of his country, directly or through freely chosen representatives. (2) Everyone has the right of equal access to public service in his country. (3) The will of the people shall be the basis of the authority of government; By genuine elections which shall be by universal and equal suffrage...";

- Article #1, states," All human beings are born Free and Equal in dignity and Rights. They are endowed with reason and conscience and should act towards one another in a spirit of brotherhood."

- Article #8, says, "Everyone has the Right to an effective Remedy by the competent national Tribunals for acts violating Fundamental Rights granted him by Constitution and by law."

**THE ALONE TONIGHT...**I don't want to live with the alone to night feeling lost at home on my own in droves of emotional plight, at times I don't know why my heart feels so blue, I suppose it's why I am so into you?

- ## **GOT TO GET CLOOOSER... TO YOU BAAABY...!**

Being here alone this night and so many before it was a disappearance of my unforgiving resistance to take hold of "splintered-family-relations" usurped in the travel of increased distances; The propensity to engage my own heart-felt sensitivities its intensity struck the chords of a hark-back, and, here I go again straddling the fence! Could there be an amenity to cross-over into the 'good and plenty?' Because what was once stuck in the shade treacled like the sweetness of marmalade or, sour-grapes bursting bottles fomenting wine-cellar brigades.

I don't want to live with the alone to night feeling lost at home on my own in droves of heart-rending plight, at times I don't know why my headaches make me feel blue, I suppose it's why I need to be so into you?

- ## **GOT TO GET CLOOOSER...TO YOU BAAABY...!**

Yet, when my mind is bereaved I leave to greet unforgiving streets which can snatch you backward, ready-or-not, my time with me once again, without shivers nor quivers, just an "all-over-me" which I cannot see! Oh, soft-pliant landing touch of dusk in moon-light caressing me marooned escalated in-sighted. My prayers were taught to me by Jonah, a four page disclaimer in potent prose "It is' I' the core of me that must be recognized..."

- Article #16, in pertinent parts, "Men and Women of full age, without any limitation due to race, nationality, or religion, have the right to marry and to found a Family, they are entitled to Equal Rights; (3) The Family is the Natural and Fundamental group Unit of Society and is entitled to protections by society and the State.

- Article #19, says, "Everyone has the right to Freedom of opinion and expression; This right includes freedom to hold opinions without interference and to seek, receive,and impart information and Ideas through any Media and Regardless of Frontiers.

- Article #23, states, "(3) Everyone has the right to just and favorable remuneration ensuring for himself and his Family an existence worthy of human dignity, and supplemented if necessary, by other means of social protection."

I don't want live with the alone tonight feeling no doubt at home on my own in droves of, now, a shift giving spirited-uplift! And at times I don't know why my essence feels so blue, I suppose it's why I am so into you?

- ## **<u>GOT TO GET CLOOOSER...TO YOU BAAABY!</u>**

All the while my words compel a storied carousel shouting-out in rapid course against opposition, the mirrored crowds all-about, ready-or-not, what shall I do? Step lively, my feet anchored to what's needed and shall not be moved! And should I die it would be the bemoaned "cries of psyche-super-fly" Ahhh, the echoed-chorus orated broken throated, I choked-back on the clutch before giving-up too much, it's the burning days, months, years of loneliness, lost souls to confusion, lost souls to beatings by the abnormal ques the young being abused, while the women lost their choice, who are you to take away their voice? To leave our children unprotected is the worse sign of the times, an oncoming impetus that must be remedied by Humanity. And though fighting gallantly as the arid air was coasting with floating-wings of the gossamer in flight through the night, thus, reckoned with the right love we can conquer anything!!!

As I stand before the unknown it dawns an open thrown pass-the baton- into the living wells of my being seeking to be righted, and let no-one deny it, this be the time to emphasize it!

- Article #11, states, "Everyone charged with a penal offense has the right to be presumed "Innocent" until proved guilty according to the law in a public trial at which he has had all the guarantees necessary for his defense. (2) No one shall be held guilty of any penal offense on account of any act or omission which did not constitute a penal offense, under national and international laws, at the time it was committed, Nor shall a heavier penalty be imposed than the one that was applicable at the time the penal offense was committed.

- Article #12, says, "No-One shall be subjected to arbitrary interference with his privacy, family, home, or correspondence, nor to attacks upon his honor and reputation. Everyone has the right to the protection of the law against such interference or attacks.

- Article #10, states, "Every-one is entitled to a fair and public hearing by independent and impartial Tribunal, in the determination of his Rights and Obligations...;

- Article #29, says, "Everyone has duties to the commitment in which alone the Free and Full development of his Personality as possible. (2) In the exercise of his rights and freedoms everyone shall be subjected only to such limitations as are determined by law solely for the purpose of securing due recognition and respect for the rights and freedoms of others, and of meeting the Just requirements of Morality, Stability, Order, and, the general welfare in a democratic society. (3) These Rights and Freedoms may in no case be exercised contrary to the purpose and Principles of the United Nations.

**THE ALONE TONIGHT...**I don't want to live with the alone tonight "feeling strengthened at home on my own in droves of upright," at times I don't know why my heart feels so blue, I suppose that's why I am so into you?

## GOT TO GET CLOOOSER...TO YOU BAAABY...!

These times are immemorial drawing near unto us-all the songs which play to their own proclaims are causing spiritual disdain, so, no-fiddling-on the roof. It's the brains-domain to sustain liquefied-lightning the "quick-quivers-slow shivers-synaptic stilled by awe" though vibrated stood-up each hairy prick in the mix, stoned-shook-off like reeds of a sycamore tree, churned honey-comb sealed in the mind beyond annals of time-sublime my heart and mind! A stirring–warbling-bustling heredity a toss-up in enormity shimmy-shine electric-eclectic-fantastic! Just too-slick for an implement, yet, its possibility clarity a win-win for the moment of "Immediate Changes!"

**THE ALONE TONIGHT...**I don't want to live with the alone tonight feeling haggard-stolid, yet, sailing upon the edges of Humanity as the Known is our Reality. And I am at home on my own in droves of 'Inner-Spright' bringing me near each time I don't know why I feel so blue, I suppose it's why I am so into you?

- ## <u>GOT GET CLOOOSER...TO YOU BAAABY...!</u>

And just like ski-falls wetted pelts of raindrops torrenchial-beautiful soaking a stony-labyrinth while clinched to the core of its own fountain-spring of inner-ascending! Oh, what a glancing-blow into my six-senses is it the "Alone Tonight" that's in plight crushing all my defenses? It assail likened to a slow-petering movement of stalking-shadows easing across plains, cataracts, and meadows with swooning Larks their tail feathers plume and colorfully bright, symbolic, to my spirits test and humanity being put to the survival of its endowment with human rights unrest!!!

- ## <u>GOT TO GET CLOOOSER...TO YOU BAAABY!</u>

- Article #25, states, " (2) Motherhood and childhood are entitled to special care and assistance, All children whether born in or out of wedlock, shall enjoy the same social Protections."

- Article #18, says, "Everyone has the right to freedom of thought, conscience...; And freedom to change his religion or belief and freedom either alone or, with community with others public or private, to manifest his religion or belief in teaching, practice, worship, and Observance.

- Article #26, states, "Everyone has the right to education...; Education shall be directed to the full development of the human personality and to the strengthening of respect for human rights and fundamental freedoms. It shall promote understanding, tolerance, and friendships among all nations, racial, or religious groups, and shall further the activities of the United Nations for the Maintenance of Peace!

Article #30, states, " Nothing in this **DECLARATION** may be interpreted as implying for any State, group, or person any right to engage in any activity asto perform any act aimed at the destruction of any Rights and Freedoms set forth **HEREIN.**

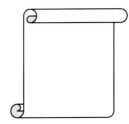

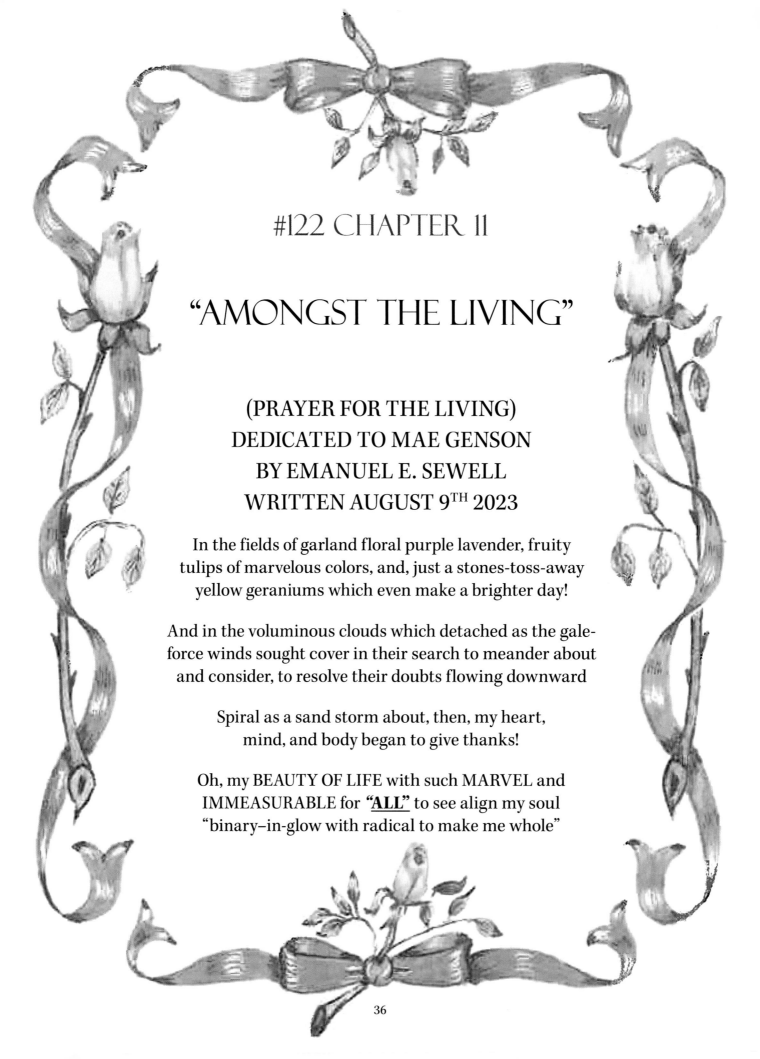

# #122 CHAPTER 11

# "AMONGST THE LIVING"

### (PRAYER FOR THE LIVING)
### DEDICATED TO MAE GENSON
### BY EMANUEL E. SEWELL
### WRITTEN AUGUST 9TH 2023

In the fields of garland floral purple lavender, fruity tulips of marvelous colors, and, just a stones-toss-away yellow geraniums which even make a brighter day!

And in the voluminous clouds which detached as the gale-force winds sought cover in their search to meander about and consider, to resolve their doubts flowing downward

Spiral as a sand storm about, then, my heart, mind, and body began to give thanks!

Oh, my BEAUTY OF LIFE with such MARVEL and IMMEASURABLE for "**ALL**" to see align my soul "binary–in-glow with radical to make me whole"

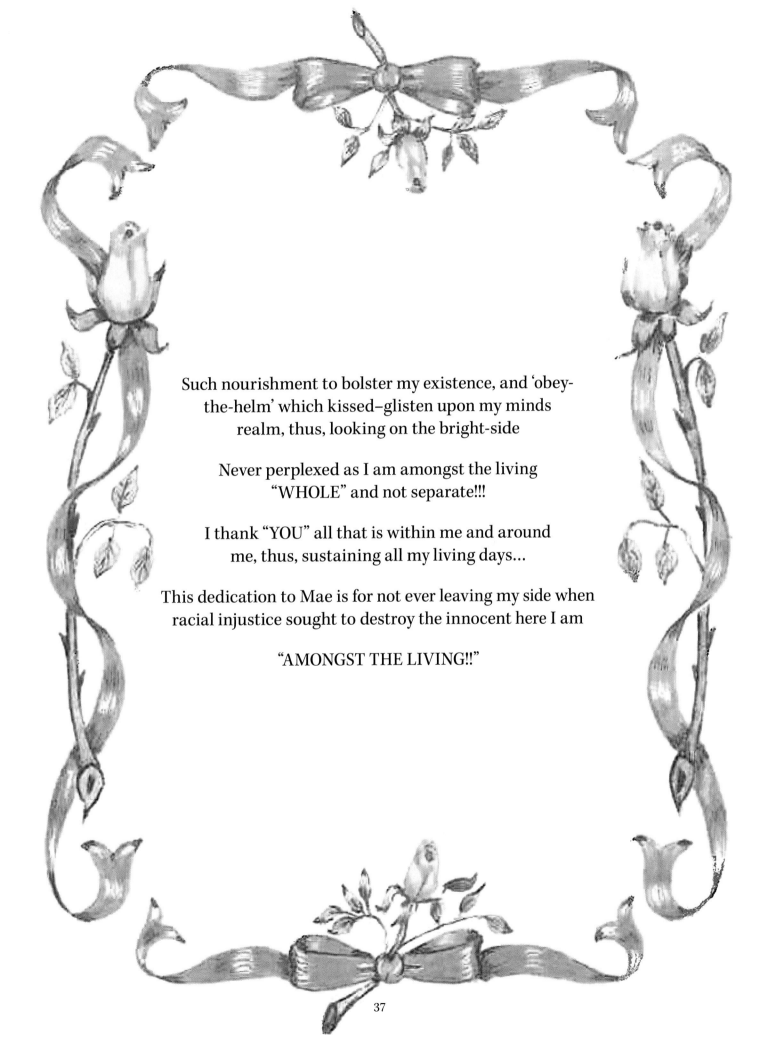

Such nourishment to bolster my existence, and 'obey-
the-helm' which kissed–glisten upon my minds
realm, thus, looking on the bright-side

Never perplexed as I am amongst the living
"WHOLE" and not separate!!!

I thank "YOU" all that is within me and around
me, thus, sustaining all my living days...

This dedication to Mae is for not ever leaving my side when
racial injustice sought to destroy the innocent here I am

"AMONGST THE LIVING!!"

# #108 CHAPTER 12

# "MOTIVATION…"

## By Emanuel E. Sewell
### Written 11-03-22 to 11-07-22

Through the misty haze of the earth's meet up with the 'magistrate of magma' a coordinating prism ensued magenta. And until the ends of time any alliance with watery sulfurs has no end…Oh, smashing and rolling currents outstretched ensconced sipping retreating edges back into the watery blue and aqua-marine scaling the shoreline prestine to usurp all that churns seaside alive or misdirected slipping-in and out again signaling to sand-dunes Just recede your heights while smoothing beaches down for "invisible footsteps" searching human plights…Ahhh-Beaches!

Yet, once the palling skies cast forth wonders paralleling its unearthing thunders that shake each uniformed "grounds of swell" profound, thus, its resounding "nell" opening its magnifying cores while shaking hands with "the world's mantle" exacting changes as we go, then choosing a justified path of perplexity by distal design! Oh marvel not this pulsing baritone the chords of the "DIVINE." To shadow mind-picturing while calling upon its pursuits crossing the frayed bows of inclination! And still tossing about mighty wet sources capering around a storm to coalesce all-humanity clearing away its desire to prowl in haste, yet, proclaim what we need without jest,

A beckoning call to **"MOTIVATION"** heave…hooo…
heave…hooo up…up…and away we go!

**"Though in its elusive and impenetrable moments reaching to saturate voices in an octaves shiver of sensational choices…"**

## *ALL THE ENDS OF THE EARTH HOVERING SPIKES OF MOTIVATION... SPARKS AND LAVA PLUME AS RAINBOWS RESUME...

Looming stolid the all encompassing moment pressing before
my vision shaken to my core with sudden indecision?

And as I walked upon a 'platinum dime' (A woman so...
so...fine and matured of mind...),

and like a sultan-sluice-wetted into the winding capes
of storms struck my resolve in waves!

She was born after my time "majestic" and uniformed
clusters of power within me chortled;

Surely, a levy of love burst sinewing bevied 'dally no more at the water's edge' grant
me this succession authentic atonement. Please do not imbue my mind during
this chivalrous time, it's a multi-dimensional search for an inward approach.

## "ALL THE ENDS OF THE EARTH HOVERING SPIKES OF MOTIVATION...THE MAGISTRATE OF MAGMA SPARKS AND LAVA PLUME AS RAINBOWS RESUME!!!"

**\*Though in its elusive and flexible moments reaching to saturate
voices in an octaves quiver of sensational choices.**

**"MOTIVATION..."**

# CHAPTER 13

# MANUSCRIPT OF LIFE STORY

### "CHRONICLES OF EMANUEL"

Here I am at precipice of my life where do I go from "a living hell?" Perhaps the dawning of days, hours, years, and decades gone by will somehow turn-the-page, where I have acknowledged the good that has come to me while at the same time punishing pains from the evil that resides in Montgomery County Maryland. And were it not for its counter parts (the department of corrections, parole/probation, and wicked court systems..), meaning, over 27 and a half years gone just petered away where I a captive even in my freedom! How the hell does this keep happening? A Donald trump law that says,"all returning citizens to society have no constitutional rights etc." And even where a chief judges order sua sponte motions hearing for the plaintiff (case #485714-V), meaning the Defendant's et. al. are in bad faith; the Attorney General admits, "extrinsic fraud" and judges who had nothing to do with the case completely ignore the law. Mind you, to contravene the Chief Judge is "CIVIL CONTEMPT" and requires swift actions to help the plaintiff Emanuel E. Sewell. The constant failure to ascertain and effectuate the law after you have been guaranteed your "exonerations" is one of the most dehumanizing and sadistic acts perpetuated by Attorney general, medical, and court officials who all used misrepresentation of rights using gang members to work as security and handle court files (The most dangerous and dumbest things ever "racketeers toss up"), legal files for anyone! If the price is right and the RICO FEDERAL LAW MEANS NOTHING ANYMORE.

Granted people were trying to help but kept being met with gang member resistance. Here I am one man fighting against corruption from all phases of where the relief comes as well. Once granted the first August 25th 2021 HEARING NOTICE providing (PROTECTION AND PUNITIVE DAMAGES), subsequently, was electrocuted by a faulty tens machine that was used excessively! So, on September 16th and 18th 2021 these electrocutions were intentional in every way, why was there no investigation after the court was made aware and provided medical records of severely injured plaintiffs? To include the Attorney general talked to the plaintiff on September 10th 2021 after she was given "VOUCHER PAYMENTS IN MY NAME BY STATE TREASURY CLAIMS DIRECTOR", THEN QUESTION PLAINTIFF ABOUT THE INCIDENTS THE INJURED HIM AT PATUXENT INSTITUTE, mind you, the plaintiff had been forced to remain in a mental institution where there was no rational justification to hold him there.

Now he suffers from strained ligaments of c1-c2-c3 of cervical spine, degenerating disc of thoracic, severe impingement of lumbar spine, and two tears in the rotator cuff. How in the world could "tendonitis" in the right shoulder amount to that much damage if it were not intentional misconduct? Were it not for pain medications, muscle relaxers, and Precision Orthopedics of laurel Maryland death and complete paralysis would have taken over my body; Then ROSM, INC. Office manager must have been an ANGEL SENT FROM HEAVEN! Because had she not intervened on my behalf I would have no ability to walk or be able to sit-up right now! And have continued to work with me even as Precision Orthopedics is no longer in my insurance network suddenly (July 26th 2023). And Interfaith Works Housing Project, Vocational Project are the most BEAUTIFUL PEOPLE! Who not only helped me three(3) times to get my health back by "MEDICAL NECESSITY." The board of Directors have a fail safe method to help all severely injured clients, my most sincere gratitude and loving appreciation to them "ALL" known and unknown.

So, now I ponder, wait and still my soul by the contracting grip of my life sitting here with so many unknown yet I fight on though my core reality weary even as fire be shut up in my bones.

I shall not ever be moved off my rock it's the "Beautiful Immeasurable" which sustains me in this very moment so that all the LOVE IN ME be freed from sinister wicked deeds against me.

# #77 CHAPTER 14

# "A MISTY SHEEN OF WHAT ADORE YOU MEANS?"

**By Emanuel E. Sewell**
**Written 4-10-22 to 2-2-23**

A frost to a brand new start, the misty sheen of what does adore you mean?

You a serene mind in me with the "good and plenty" so sweet
into you, is why my aching heart careens blue,

and the ribbon flails anew, it would be a bonnet singing out melodic sonnets.

Let the years of searing un-dried tears bearing the
untold become stolid in the heart so bold!

It was caressed by a sheen screen of misty haze drift of what caught my tiring eye's?

An adoring sift as in turning my haste leaning around a stony labyrinth;

Ahhh...My love above and between "us" it was gravity who bequeath
the seams of our true inner means, is that all I need?

**\*A MISTY SHEEN OF WHAT DOES ADORE YOU MEAN ?**

A cherry blossom within two heart's/minds absent branches no chance for
happenstance and that, which shielded our spirits blended into the cove, thus at
first glance the dove arose, so, mend swelter of your breath around penetrate true
intentions and within the octave of your chants pure taste, a garden of romance...

What was once thought to be a spiritual coffin, became
the bended knees of quiet sensitivity.

Now, alive clutched into the mind just a little too much without my caressing touch.

And had it been an "earthquake" contemplating its quiver-quiet-quick shivers have
a heart in me "Shake-N-Bake" before it's too late...up...up...up each spirit awakes!

### *A MISTY SHEEN OF WHAT DOES ADORE YOU MEAN ?

Thus, green acres supplied slippery lilacs muster's which covered
custard and searched for the road paved in gold:

**"Red Rover...Red Rover... stroke the lavender furs of purple
clovers plush...pliant reached clothed upon the plant world "sweet
nectar aroma pleasant gossomered sooth...night entreat! Ahhh...
Young Man...Ahhh... a sensual plate for my palate's sake."**

RISE...RISE...RISE...! Were it not for the love above and between
"us" our remembrance would be drowned in empty rivers.

Oh, save "us" before the sacred breath leaves the "heart's crest," the horizontal
glow at the edge of what our hearts' and minds intend to know!

### *A MISTY SHEEN OF WHAT DOES ADORE YOU MEAN...

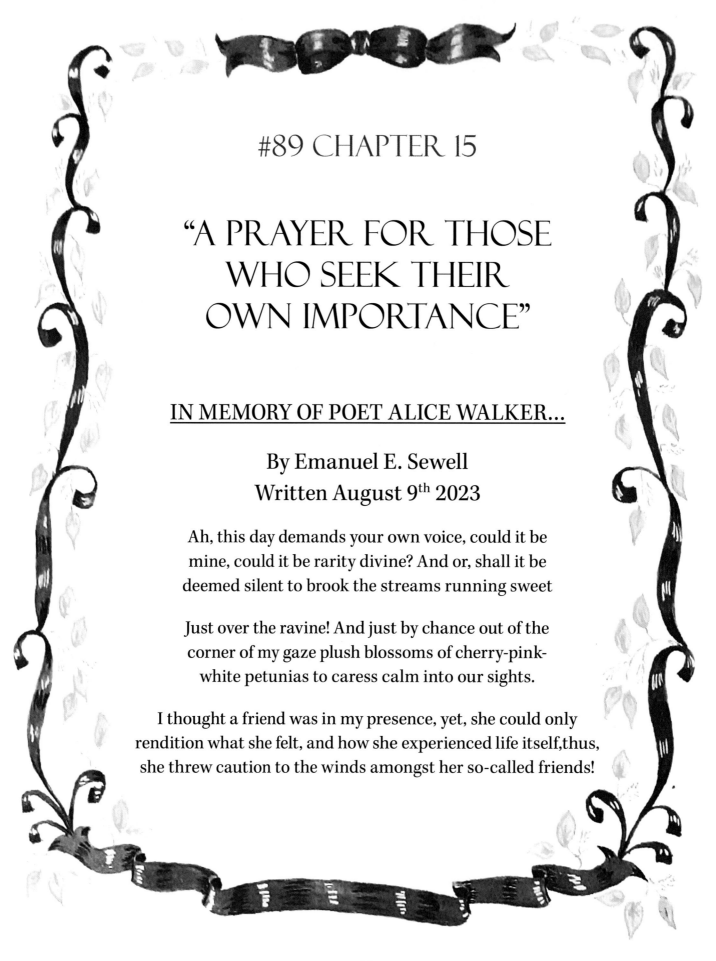

# #89 CHAPTER 15

# "A PRAYER FOR THOSE WHO SEEK THEIR OWN IMPORTANCE"

## IN MEMORY OF POET ALICE WALKER...

By Emanuel E. Sewell
Written August 9th 2023

Ah, this day demands your own voice, could it be mine, could it be rarity divine? And or, shall it be deemed silent to brook the streams running sweet

Just over the ravine! And just by chance out of the corner of my gaze plush blossoms of cherry-pink-white petunias to caress calm into our sights.

I thought a friend was in my presence, yet, she could only rendition what she felt, and how she experienced life itself,thus, she threw caution to the winds amongst her so-called friends!

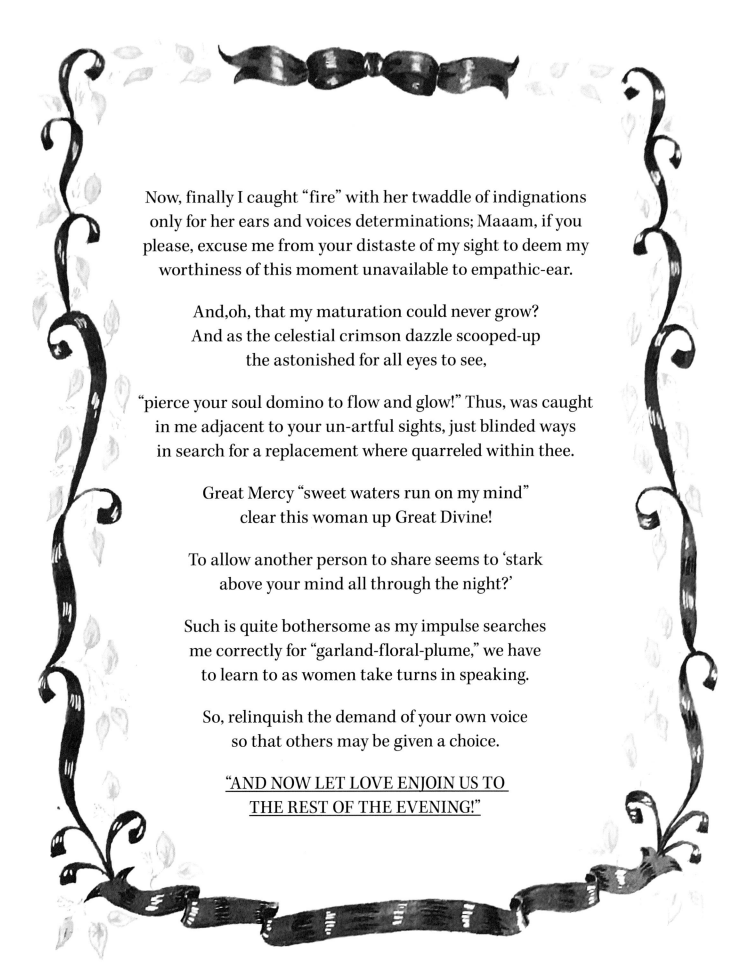

Now, finally I caught "fire" with her twaddle of indignations
only for her ears and voices determinations; Maaam, if you
please, excuse me from your distaste of my sight to deem my
worthiness of this moment unavailable to empathic-ear.

And,oh, that my maturation could never grow?
And as the celestial crimson dazzle scooped-up
the astonished for all eyes to see,

"pierce your soul domino to flow and glow!" Thus, was caught
in me adjacent to your un-artful sights, just blinded ways
in search for a replacement where quarreled within thee.

Great Mercy "sweet waters run on my mind"
clear this woman up Great Divine!

To allow another person to share seems to 'stark
above your mind all through the night?'

Such is quite bothersome as my impulse searches
me correctly for "garland-floral-plume," we have
to learn to as women take turns in speaking.

So, relinquish the demand of your own voice
so that others may be given a choice.

"AND NOW LET LOVE ENJOIN US TO
THE REST OF THE EVENING!"

# #113 CHAPTER 16

# "LEAN ME INTO LOVE…SHINE…SHINE!"

### By Emanuel E. Sewell
### Written 11-8-22

O, call back the eternal landscapes of what lasts where a time has come and in its enormity each stirring fountain spring spewing forth from the core of the earth, the momentous proximate of springing coils in combination with each memory of mankind.

"On a cold blistering sheath of the day bolstered my anchored world to freeze its natural phenomena as it ebbs into the 'womb of time,' thus, bidding its return within the souls urn!"

**\*LEANNN…ME INTOOO…LOVE…SHINE…SHINE WHAT PROPELS ME!**

And I just so happen to lift tired watery eyes as my head raised with a search into clear blue skies above me; Lo, a hawk-back raptor with its wings drown-in just a tad to suck-in each feral circuited sail and its eyes set to the level of hulk so precise such vision demanded all your attentions as it perused atop the forestry canopy gliding in from its perch of oscillating approach (A 5,550 ft. high) and with such grace a soaring chase, and oh, that the

"HEAVENS-Curtained-Glaze" kissed its wings into amaze! And as each sighted clinch of its talons began to sway

Into 'segued slants' the raptor saw its chance. The gossamer-wings of life ignited burning churns as if it were a beaming torch! In which the azure skyline was stung still from casting gleams of glistening out of the release of radiant flow ever glowing!

Then the mutual objective was instinctively accepted where 'mother natures' help to feed its broods thus turning another page, as if in final lerch torpedoing in downward spiral to pounce.

Just at this time of visioning and mental venturing pressing hard upon my own life's personal inquiry?

And although I had an endorsement of simultaneous embracing (A new lady friend met..), it also became an initial challenge to redefine this arduous journey, can I solemnly pledge that which has put my life upon a precipice (Not knowing whether things will last or go bad?)

Yet, leans me onward to a pathway saturated with the alliance of human rigors, and, is the greatest inclination to re-ignite my true mission.

**\*LEANN…ME INTOOO…LOOOVE…SHINE…SHINE WHAT PROPELS ME!**

## #2 CHAPTER 17

# "COLORFUL DIMENSIONS... MY CHILDREN!"

**By Emanuel E. Sewell
Written 12-4-22 to 07-29-22**

Just sitting in a stung glance as phrases, words and silence emerge
to fill the lines of this festive moment where my grandchildren,

Caleb A.K.A Lil Hano, Alana A.K.A Love Muffin, and Michael A.K.A
Poncho bring my cockle edged heart into atonement and shall I gauge
its total effect. It would be the scampering of my spirit reaching out to
them in "one fell stroke" of what a grandfather's heart invokes...

Though the curtains sway from the oscillating churns of
the ceiling fan while mother nature on the other-side of my
sliding glass patio door echoed back a light rumble,

a grumble or two just to get me in my night time grooves.

All my memories of Lil hano never fade away my first born, even now that he's a
young man about to graduate high school, none of our plans have come true,

Building blocks for train set, building volcanoes with baking soda,
and all his little traps he likes from when he was left home alone by
himself the same as I went through when being his age too;

**\*BEING SHOCKED IN A WORLD OF WONDER DOES NOT
ALLOW FOR ME TO FEEL THE EARTH'S THUNDER ?**

**Then love muffin is born it seems that looking at her picture just
does not suffice; Where is the synchronized smile with glee,**

**an animated touch where her arms find a way around my neck ? All
those moments alone without me, could very well spell doubt!**

**Yeah, who is granddad and why can I not share cooking French
Toast with him or, just eat some yogurt to palate my thirst.**

**And just when I thought all gems were no-longer being sprung
from their Mom, her comes Poncho my second baby boy,**

**who has several of my features baring on me not having dentures.**

**The spectacular thing about it all is that I cannot stop smiling
thinking of being there for them somehow…someway…
Like the churning dials of the sun to heat the day**

**As my children play,thus, they are ever kissed in my reminisce, and, just as I
was in jolt a flash of an lightning bolt struck the skies in down-pour harmonize,
then, a sizzle-chisel-pop struck the earth as I felt my family in its search!!!**

**\*Colorful Dimensions…And my grandchildren got my Attention.**

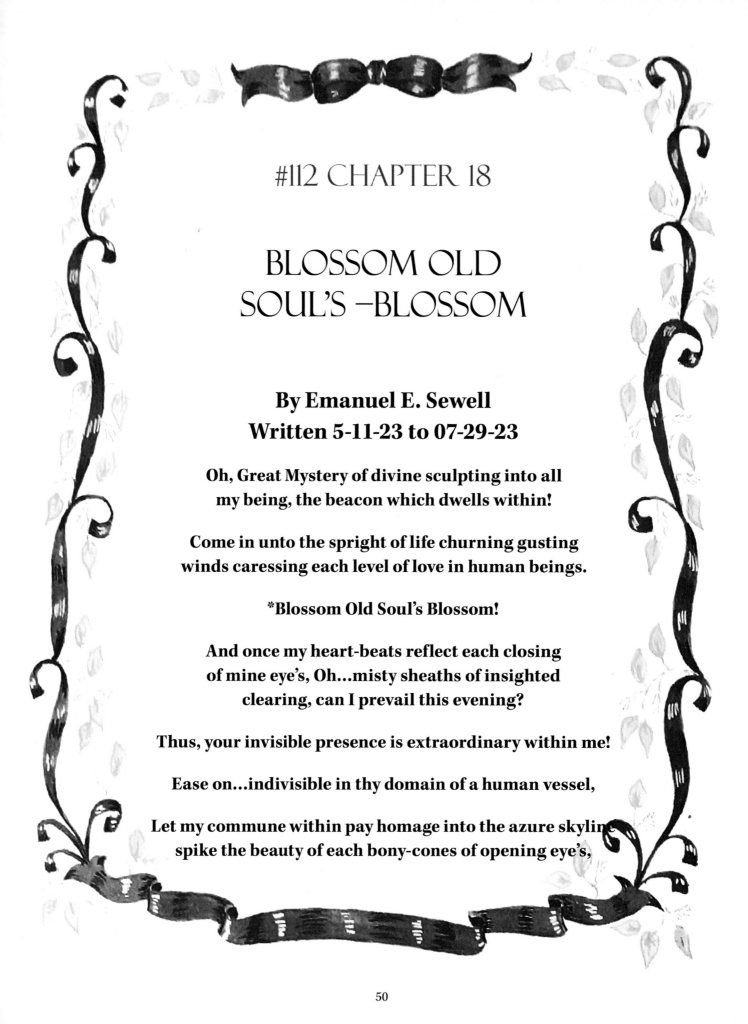

#112 CHAPTER 18

# BLOSSOM OLD SOUL'S —BLOSSOM

**By Emanuel E. Sewell**
**Written 5-11-23 to 07-29-23**

Oh, Great Mystery of divine sculpting into all
my being, the beacon which dwells within!

Come in unto the spright of life churning gusting
winds caressing each level of love in human beings.

*Blossom Old Soul's Blossom!

And once my heart-beats reflect each closing
of mine eye's, Oh...misty sheaths of insighted
clearing, can I prevail this evening?

Thus, your invisible presence is extraordinary within me!

Ease on...indivisible in thy domain of a human vessel,

Let my commune within pay homage into the azure skyline
spike the beauty of each bony-cones of opening eye's,

even as scudding darkened clouds begin to spread-out,
to kiss crimson haze into sparkling crystals of amaze!

Thus, cast upon the 'gardens frost' a simmering
chorus before us wrapped in the divine of mind-
picturing, an escapade into swaying green glades;

Soft sooth my inner strength and joy sipped
ahead of my present testaments!

*Blossom Old Soul's Blossom!

-Let brevity in prayer be thy strength as
joy testifies to our enlivenment.

# "PLUSH GREENS-SOOTHE THE SOUL-NO SUPERFICIAL MODE!!!"

**By Emanuel E. Sewell**
**Written 10-11-21 to 9-4-22 to 11-5-22...**

**It's the fading squint of prop-perfections moving in precision, soft and surrendered reasons sky-frost falling being seasonally sifted...**And thus, a stream of white clusters intensified its determined locations.

Oh, how pleasant each grapple with a fact as all colorful designs
by downcast of drifting clouds petering shears of shaven-sheaves,
thus the enormity of sheaths blanket an unknown?

The emptying alive of fluffed-up skyscrapers shuffling-in from the blown gales
an eastward force to touch each patch of 'tilled swelter' onward search...

And although no sunny gleams appeared its crystal-glisten caressed its melting moods easing away flailing from the perch unto all the ends of where waters were frozen in wetted diversions, the "secreted away" drifting upon an echoes pulse, signaling the sacred gathering which stilled blind-intentions in the acidic-bubble of my appetites it took water to sooth my concentric-unctions, an undeniable 'legend-superstar' all the days of its coming in "Illumined" reinvention was dropped a pearl that shimmied my world!

Yes, all-around me are needs in degrees as the night was brushed and salted white-wet by exalting and exhaling thrashing winds of snow mixed with rain, when it's cold outside who are you holding?

What was once thought to be transparent stood stolid and was scaled by an orchestration of prone-poise encouraging 'chivalrous pleas' just for

"good-minds-sake" all that appeared to be stung into silence broke free from quivering lips, thus, the lighthouse strobing beams lit off a ghost streaming teal of that which delights us most its coptered-capture of the east-coast trembling in its quake surely it would be time to embrace!

## PLUSH GREENS-SOOTHE THE SOUL-NO SUPERFICIAL MODE...

In the diagonal positions where the earth's rotations stood in remission, just a sparkle of rhinestone hidden in the frosting bush 'honey-suckle-sweet' a treacle of the cool tinted mission to further our greets, and that, the night... wafted with each scent of lightly brushed daffodils by trailing gusting-circuits...all my soul in levitation as I watched churning waters.

I prefer to ease-up just enough to clutch-on into the positing-posture of my words, lit-ablaze I pray sending a vision as it parted out of the haze, thus, a new company arise horizontal amaze! Now is the time of our sensitivity that we soil our views mentioned with brevity;

And it's time not to take too long 'pitty-patting upon the garden's frost,' it must be magic 'cause it feels so good to meee...must be love-must be love in yooou? Oh, it must be magic cause it feels so good to meee...must be love-must be love in yooou!"

Yes, tend to my reservoir of heartaches as I await your pure tastes wherein bordered nooks of tasty treats provide meaningful moments to sincerely meet.

As the sweetness of your human meekness is where I found a Queen with a crown revealed in uniqueness. It was the soulful moorings of my being which set the reveal in cruise-control, a testament of what has been shared about our dreams becoming the "Imminent Works" in the rigors of life keeping me up…countless…sleepless nights, and just, like flowers needing sun and rain "alive again from what the storms chased in!"

## PLUSH GREENS-SOOTHE THE SOUL-NO SUPERFICIAL MODE…

**IF THERE EVER WAS A GENIE IN A BOTTLE…**The gift of a wish…The gift of a wish…Into a great gift of My Queen of quiet means as I am only human subject to the realms of let's make it last. And am tested, tried, with truth,so, why hold back from this 'souls-natural-aphrodisiac?' I've searched the oceans with the crashing currents winding into thrashing sulfur waves of the sea, for the 'cranning-hook-of-love' just above…just because…and just beyond compare, would you comfort my passionate gaze and still be there? Let's try to patch-it-all-up!

We can settle the dust pushing upon our trust, thus, course the anticipation while crumbling the core of hesitation; On came the road paved in eucalyptus design 'pillow-posh sweet' scented with love without the need for interlocking between wooden lattices. And oh, what a treat my hourglass-figurine, a mahogany-honey-brown just a sweeter taste of life, could you one day be my wife? Be not blinded by the gold-untold handle the exclusive degrees of attention simmering at our growth allowing us to move closer we need to know.

So, peel-back the once closed doors of a "broken heart" heal into one's own hearts' a woven-fabric-seal to mesh frayed seams by bending to one knee cherishes the moments of what "true love" really means.

## PLUSH GREENS-SOOTHE THE SOUL-NO SUPERFICIAL MODE!!!

"IN THE PULSATING NOURING DAYS OF A MOMENT RESONATE, 'IT IS SOUND THAT SINEWS INTO HUMAN AND ALL LIFE!'

ITS RENEWING FORCE EXCHANGES 'MOTHER-NATURES' CHOICE, THUS, BEING RESTORED CAN BE A HEALING POTION AND REMEMBERED DEVOTION. THE VIBRATING TUNES OF ALL LIFE GRANTS SUCH A BENEFIT-THERAPEUTIC…"

# #35 CHAPTER #20

# "THE ENDURED"

## By Emanuel E. Sewell
## Written 7-12 and 13 to 7-25-23

In the mornings whisked phase of fair-weather misty drips kiss my face as a moment of atoning, how long shall you leave me lonely? Because my mind is unclear about the suffering year after year all legal paperwork is clear; Yet the minutes, hours, months peter into a living misery while I am trying to fashion life anew! Can barely stand watching lifting dusk as somehow in this day "the endured" shall prevail and improve what's left even where I search high and low, where is the 'sugar and spice' that's to follow my Glow?

This day is a blessing which my Sweet Mother Beauty without Measure wash over me quick-quiet needs a hidden power upon the thickets stretchout THY HANDS,as I am trying to peer into the one thing found in you? That was never there with my own flesh and blood of no mother. Thus I am thunder struck by the details in my view though I never ever allow oneself to get too down 'life goes on even with the rain and silent storms.' What do I have to do assail suave with effortless moves that only shine in spiritual highlight, as my body is continuously in physical plight, as my nerves sometimes supercede my senses feeling like I am becoming unglued!

And should YOU approach with subtle versatile ways as the wise during extraodinary times it's my humble gaze which allows me to brook warm sentiment even where I wonder, why is this? And oh, that the bones of my chilled body come back to form ease on closer into the masked benefit that life is still generating through me, and not being pelted by superficial intentions. Where is the "UNION THE UNBREAKABLE BONDS?" My focus genuinely clear to find that ONE THING IN YOU!

The moment so intense to just lift the veil without <u>"show and tell",</u>
<u>this be an intricate lesson pantomimed wetted incursion into</u>
<u>dynamic views "all of heaven bequeathed inside of you!</u>

Where the stones of the earth anchor my position every hour of my living, should there be a preferable rainbow of prism in which the 'glowing dial's helm caressed your force and source shone-in glisten?' I have thought many times I had accomplished my mission "ENDURED" and learning from the mysterious generous...

And where the seagulls glide above ocean waves, rolling currents,
and stillness while the skies illusions of blue, mauve, and
crimson (The Tindal Affect-Bony-cones of our eyes.)

What a surprise! And just to think our world never absent of glee, humor, and papable times spiked-exuberant as this moment captured-endured forevermore...

### <u>"WHO OF MANKIND WOLUD ENDURE MUCH MORE?"</u>

# #27 CHAPTER 21

# "BLOSSOM OLD SOUL'S –BLOSSOM"

## PART #2 COMES AFTER PRAYER OF #112
## BLOSSOM OLD SOUL'S- BLOSSOM...

## By Emanuel E. Sewell
## Written On 1-28-23 to 07-28-23

Thy wonders "Beautiful Immeasurable" ...tether me sweet ...tether me keen...tether me in the morning so that my hearts' be serene!

Thus, flush me clean where the earth's flowers seek my spirit's sheen. And return to me unbeknownst seeking thy paradise within me !

Please recover greenness and be my grasses blade in the shade calling on my moss high tower in each midst of shivering hours.

I tribute each day as a grief dripping away, just as the snow in the month's that may.

So, now a flower sprout with the casting glisten of Mother Nature's intentions;

Oh, let thy wonders shake the earth's grounds by heavens thunders, and, the pitty-patter of raindrops...slosh-pop-slosh on tree limbs and budding petals, the chime of life!

### *OH, LET THERE BE LIGHT!!!

Thus, these be wonders of love and life, slip-sliding...coool...slick...glide into the gardens of preamble-no-shambles, yet manageable tangibles, as death has no end in life.

They both make "us" see what we all could become or be nothing without its magnifying degrees to create "almost" all things.

<u>*BLOSSOM OLD SOUL'S BURN THY INNER CANDLE "TEMPEST"</u>
<u>IN THE CORE OF ITS BEST REPRESENTATION OF "US".</u>

<u>-BLOSSOM OLD SOUL'S –BLOSSOM!</u>

# #98 CHAPTER 22

# "JUST US TWO !"

## By Emanuel E. Sewell
## Written 4-16-22

Soft is the whispering ambulate gusting churns of the earth
exchanging day to criss-cross over with the night and as my mind
was blown heavens lit-up in me a picturesque scene for sure!

In the fulcrum of expance skitter-spritz dispersed the fire rings enchasing
us 'stratosphere!' Thus, mirrored with the "all-sparks" beams and pierced
its nicks in every sparkle of the vast sea, a resemblance of "Just You and Me"
heavenly begun satisfied imbued-eidetic-eclectic-enigmatic fantastic!

And for good mind-sake arose towering vapors in a distant aloof, yet, its
turning high-rising funnels capering into magnetic storms, oh that it
be stilled by nature's chain leaving brief voids being drawn into rolling-
under-currents, a crown of the world dubbed in all watery abyss!

Over the mountains and over the waves we get closer and closer in the deep-blue where
the 'Thunder Brakes' the powers of the earth meander, and, surrender to the depths
of bends nothing pretends where its lightning strikes ascend, "white hot claps of night
and day" extends before the life of 'mans fountains' and where enlivenment begins!

And just 'a stones toss away' the shoreline pelted by the crashing sulfur
unforgiving to what was creeping-down from the 'apex of wonder' shaking
the borders where landscapes flower, the "Jungle-Boogie" in clear view
cashmere-sooth my mind where brief laser-light shone through to embrace

elephant-ears precious to its colorful cousins of aquatic and exotic plant life: bird songs, bountiful raindrops, rhodondrums which tamp-down on the 'frosty-freeze' that could hold a man to his knees absent the earth's breeze…

**"JUST US TWO…JUST ME FOR YOU…"**

**"GIRL YOU KNOW-I'LL BE THERE FOR YOU & CAN PROVIDE…!"**

Thus, seeping off tree-tops while pelting nectared clovers, and paved a road in shimmy-shadow-swelter by what has just been told.

It has no hold over where the floods are the deepest and rocks are the steepest…

**"RED ROVER…RED ROVER…STROKE THE PETALS OF OCCASION CARESSING LOVE HUGGED INTO LAVENDER AS ITS FURS BENT OVER AND STUNG ITS CLOVERS! WHICH REACHED- OUT TO SNAG 'PEACH ROSES' TANGLED SCENTED BY NECTAR TO REMIND ALL PASSERS BY IT'S THE LILACS-LUSTER WHICH CLUTCHED THE ASSAILING WINDS 'ALIVE AGAIN' FROM WHAT LOVE BROUGHT IN…"**

A moment came in too much, just a 'treacle of something sweet' though you could not eat!

Hot speeding flashes of fiery lances just caressed its petals and ignited its plight! A new meet-up with the night.

A soulful trembling was me loving you…The hum…strum…of heart beat drums and croons of the moon gave a bellowing tune 'Just Me For You'

As my chords give vocal songs of our pains they go away brushed and sifted wet just like snow mixed with rain nature proclaimed its disdain we rise once again.

Great amber-host is loving you arced in an unbearable fire? And lit by the earth' shivers climbing down a lightning stalk straight way upon the spectrum of dangling blue violet indigo shoots,"crackle-snap-pop" chiseled-charred-smoked! Thus, splintered was the occasion of our human invoke searing hot seams of what new life in "us" means.

**"JUST US TWO…JUST ME FOR YOU!!!"**

# #106 CHAPTER 23

# DAFFODILS AND FRUITY CHILLS!

## By Emanuel E. Sewell
## Written 9-26-22

The fruitful companions which lay upon the stark
plains of seemingly haunted empty cannons?

It seems there's an intriguing possibility of no futility, how could
one wander lonely with so much liveliness around you?

Where each spirit of 'flighty eye catches' darting swoon-sweep-swish!
Then in and out of bushes and at times they become tangled by vines
from mangrove shoots in the thickets dangling like linguine strands,
then blending into the enormous hills sloping overlapping parts of
plateaus with hanging 'crags of rock' considered the strongest places on
earth anchored as monolith's, jagged edged cliffs, and mountain sides
all while Earth's crust protrude giant boulders of granite or, shale rock
some hard to see in the midst of mystery though back dropped into dusky
woods that cause one's eyes to strain and make your heart-beats stop!

Thus, upon my mind in the split-second of time, I felt there was an island
before me or, was I dreaming? Lo and behold a rare "PREHISTORIC
AFFAIR" here scantily-clad amongst the bush towering maybe hundreds
of feet high red cedar oaks and polka-dotted around its roots bulking up
out of the ground just around the sides and underneath it was a cite to see
dropping and pelting the soil and tree roots black walnuts skimming off
white velvety petals and bright yellow plumes of seeping wet "daffodils!"

And snagged on one of its green leafy stalks an alder branch just by chance...

Oh, my goodness over there to my immediate right a glance
of a good days nature walking, rustling in a prickly bush the
beauty of it stunning for all eyes to see and I've landed in,

"a fool's paradise" the plumage so colorful (blue, green, yellow, and gold),
this canary is rare and peeka-booing looking at me while its wings fluttering
in its clawed toe prance as if to say "this is my space watch your step young
fella!", and, still seeking what it needs (insects..) many crawling on the wetted
grounds then exiting the ancient aged old tree...up...up...skyward bound.

The heavens bellowed an echoing call royal upon the rustling-bustling flourish
of each breeze coursing through beautiful foliage as the daylight palls to fade
into the crimson horizon while the azure skyline smiled with its clouds pillowy-
puff-posh- cottony just enough even as lichen drips of hemlock its bounty
finicky where the moorings of coastal sands felt ignored yet, waters brooked
with trickling ease pressing on with the silver-sheen of the setting sun, thus,
helms of crystallite lifted life upon its high-tower and hailing threw flailing
leaflets and coptering colorful leaves to soil the hallowed grounds not a sound
for the friends lost of this season, prickly pears and poke berries in descend.

How engaging as I pass over barnacled encrusted layovers broken off of
meteorite shoulders, the berms in conflict being pounded by dropping wild
berries and lupine haversacked to hulking columns of towering tree habitat!

Such a silent delight we are 'heart bound' by mind, soul in hand
only when the spirit is in throes, while the chords of octave
serenade each day then take flight set to each hour's delight.

"BACK DOWN MEMORY LANE...AN INSTANT PHOTOGRAPH CROSSED
OVER THE THOUGHTS OF MY PAST...BACK DOWN MEMORIES LANE..."

**Daffodil's And Fruity Chills!!!**

# #55 CHAPTER 24

# "THE MOTHERLAND LET THE CHILDREN FLOW…"

## By Emanuel E. Sewell
## Written 7-03-23

Klickity-klack perhaps the throne of my home is my woman's 'PHEROMONES ?'
As it is written on her face, then, each step I take Is one to never "FORSAKE!!!"

It's the reflections of "superior powers" Ahhh, magma chambered
at the earth's core just skipped off polarity, and, a jagged lance-
sizzling-branch; And tickle –peter-piper-sip-cipher…

Oh, chill my contracting grip! In the days I layed in the shade and my hands
caressed the soul of my 'WOMAN'S' hourglass hips (Second to None.)

This is a world on the "MOTHER LAND TRIP," what do you mean?

Who of you can maternal value hunkered intersticed life into life! Only a
woman can harness 'living waters' ripple-curl-swirl into her figurine world.

All infinite be thy not contrite, labor in beauty, Be pleased
'bless my soul Domino let the children flow!!!

Oh, mystery-music-magic the buzz-hub-behold still your heart-beats
dynamic this be our world polished in its differences of man and woman
which "bridged the gap",and, isn't that the reason the "CREATOR" has

consecrated our "SOULS" adorned, individual, and gave "US" LOVE, Woman & Children the bright reflections of what and whom we "ADORE!"

TRICKLED WATERS OVER EMBEDDED STONES SHALL THE MOUNTAIN WONDER?
**THE MOON-LIT SILVER SPARKLES OFF FOUNTAIN SPRINGS**
**ECHO AS THE EARTH BALANCED HER THUNDERS**

**SNAP-CRACKLE-POP...AND A DOWNPOUR SWISH-**
**WASHED-WHISKED DOUSED BY GOOD TASTE!**

**So, counter detect, look around what's in the mix?**

1). Thoughts liquefied an embryo's chain into its Mother's
bodily domain mainly her core and the brain;

2). The things sensed when I touch her the child kicks;

3). Those of you who have no clue step a little closer into view...
Na...Na..don't try to look back (There is nothing asexual here and
no cell can be split, who are you with?) Nature abounds;

This will be the moment for all those innocent people who have died for
holding to their Natural Side, and those still alive you chime and always

"FIGHT-BACK" WE ARE THE NATURAL APHRODISIAC!!!

Our intelligence is a signal beacon letting you know that you never have to
give-up on what you already know "YOUR GENDER IS A WINGED DEFENDER"
assail high fly as binary is not a living hell its entrails are the "WHOLE HUMAN
PREVAIL..." (BINARY AND RADICAL-ATOM ACT AS ONE AND NOT SEPARATE.)

And don't make me spike the furs of a planted word, all my 'DIVINE' blossom
into the nick form everywhere the "SUN-LIGHT KISSES!!!" Upon Thee.

AHHH...maceration and ovulation will forever

"DOMINATE" my "GENERATIONS!!!

Would you be mine, Could you be mine, Will you be my "NEIGHBOR?"

BOW now, honey-suckle-sweet, since when have you not heard the good word?

And since when have we as a "HUMAN FAMILY" not trained our "HUMAN-UNCTIONS" to be "**MOTHER EARTH'S FUNCTIONS?**"

**"KLICKETY-KLACK-PERHAPS AS I WALK DOWN THE STALK OF THE HEAVENS THAT MY THRONE BE WRAPPED TO ANCHOR AND PULL-UP MY "BACK-BONE," NOW I KNOW WHERE'S HOME!!!"**

**"THE MOTHERLAND LET THE CHILDREN FLOW..."**

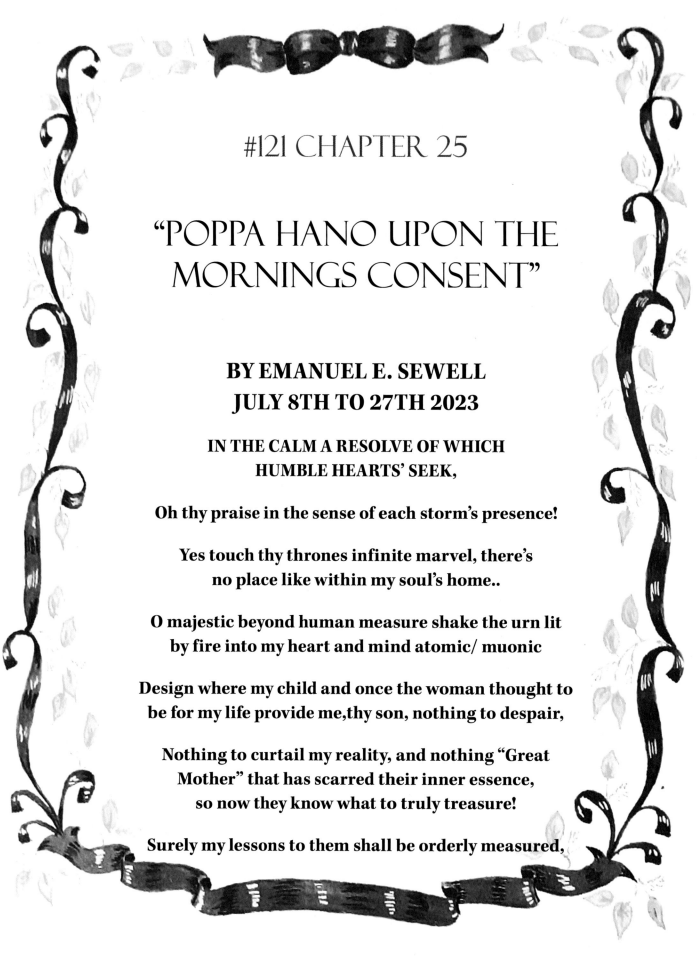

# #121 CHAPTER 25

## "POPPA HANO UPON THE MORNINGS CONSENT"

**BY EMANUEL E. SEWELL**
**JULY 8TH TO 27TH 2023**

**IN THE CALM A RESOLVE OF WHICH**
**HUMBLE HEARTS' SEEK,**

Oh thy praise in the sense of each storm's presence!

Yes touch thy thrones infinite marvel, there's
no place like within my soul's home..

O majestic beyond human measure shake the urn lit
by fire into my heart and mind atomic/ muonic

Design where my child and once the woman thought to
be for my life provide me,thy son, nothing to despair,

Nothing to curtail my reality, and nothing "Great
Mother" that has scarred their inner essence,
so now they know what to truly treasure!

Surely my lessons to them shall be orderly measured,

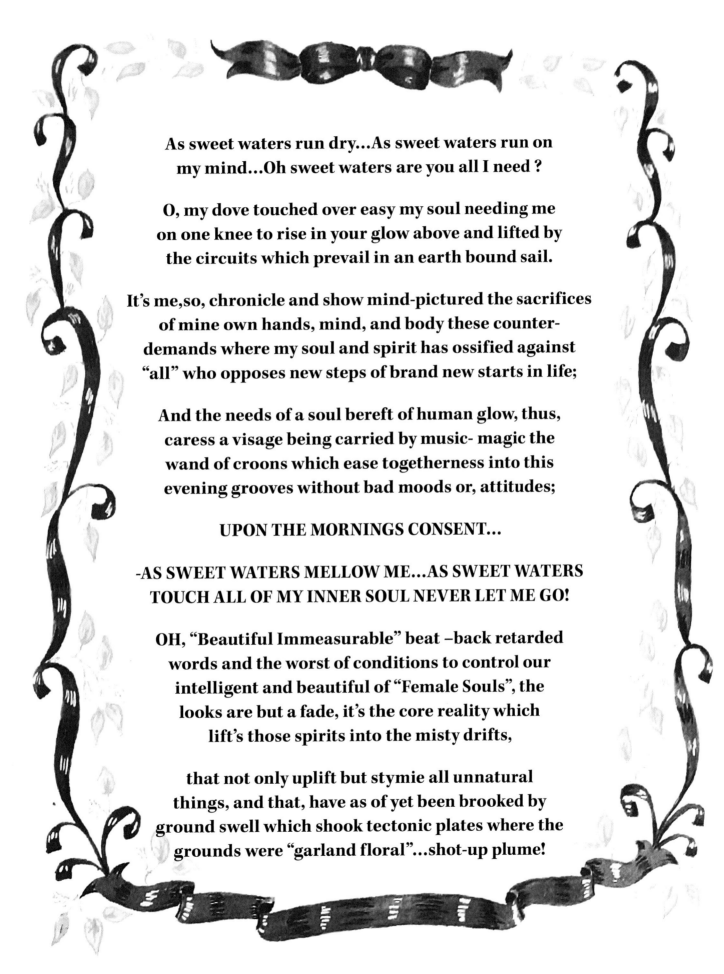

As sweet waters run dry...As sweet waters run on
my mind...Oh sweet waters are you all I need ?

O, my dove touched over easy my soul needing me
on one knee to rise in your glow above and lifted by
the circuits which prevail in an earth bound sail.

It's me,so, chronicle and show mind-pictured the sacrifices
of mine own hands, mind, and body these counter-
demands where my soul and spirit has ossified against
"all" who opposes new steps of brand new starts in life;

And the needs of a soul bereft of human glow, thus,
caress a visage being carried by music- magic the
wand of croons which ease togetherness into this
evening grooves without bad moods or, attitudes;

UPON THE MORNINGS CONSENT...

-AS SWEET WATERS MELLOW ME...AS SWEET WATERS
TOUCH ALL OF MY INNER SOUL NEVER LET ME GO!

OH, "Beautiful Immeasurable" beat –back retarded
words and the worst of conditions to control our
intelligent and beautiful of "Female Souls", the
looks are but a fade, it's the core reality which
lift's those spirits into the misty drifts,

that not only uplift but stymie all unnatural
things, and that, have as of yet been brooked by
ground swell which shook tectonic plates where the
grounds were "garland floral"...shot-up plume!

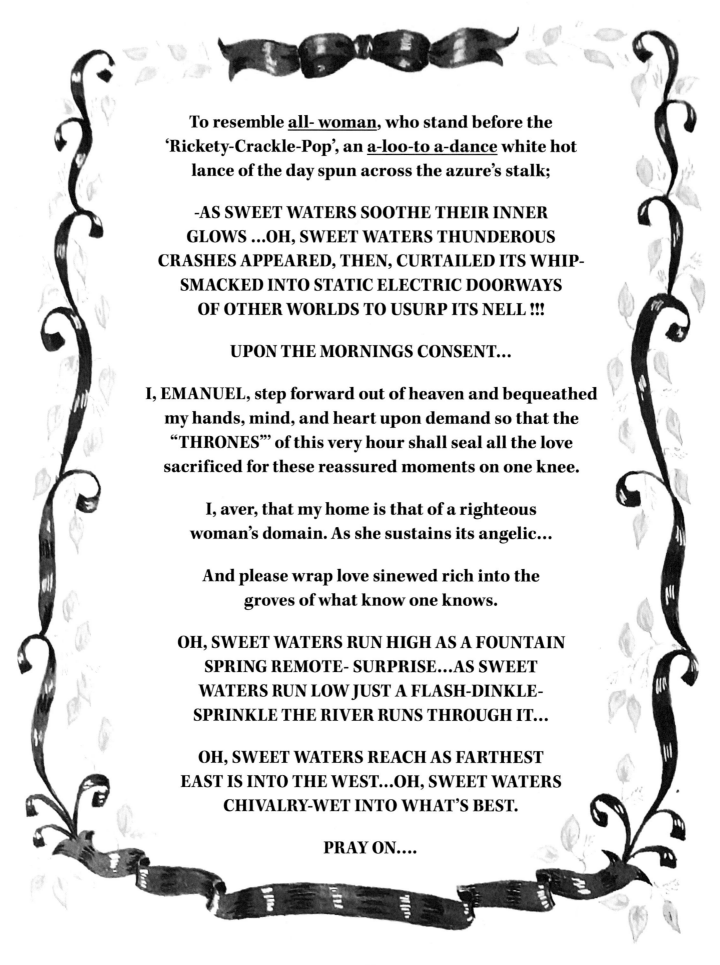

To resemble <u>all- woman</u>, who stand before the
'Rickety-Crackle-Pop', an <u>a-loo-to a-dance</u> white hot
lance of the day spun across the azure's stalk;

-AS SWEET WATERS SOOTHE THEIR INNER
GLOWS ...OH, SWEET WATERS THUNDEROUS
CRASHES APPEARED, THEN, CURTAILED ITS WHIP-
SMACKED INTO STATIC ELECTRIC DOORWAYS
OF OTHER WORLDS TO USURP ITS NELL !!!

UPON THE MORNINGS CONSENT...

I, EMANUEL, step forward out of heaven and bequeathed
my hands, mind, and heart upon demand so that the
"THRONES'" of this very hour shall seal all the love
sacrificed for these reassured moments on one knee.

I, aver, that my home is that of a righteous
woman's domain. As she sustains its angelic...

And please wrap love sinewed rich into the
groves of what know one knows.

OH, SWEET WATERS RUN HIGH AS A FOUNTAIN
SPRING REMOTE- SURPRISE...AS SWEET
WATERS RUN LOW JUST A FLASH-DINKLE-
SPRINKLE THE RIVER RUNS THROUGH IT...

OH, SWEET WATERS REACH AS FARTHEST
EAST IS INTO THE WEST...OH, SWEET WATERS
CHIVALRY-WET INTO WHAT'S BEST.

PRAY ON....

## #96 CHAPTER 26

# "CAN'T EXPLAIN IT?"

By Emanuel E. Sewell
Written 4-16-22

The shadows eclipsed…The shadows eclipsed…The shadows eclipsed wherein swirling untamed winds was coursing upon extended sprightly-lit butterfly wings silver is the sparkle in every flap where each song bird segueing;

Should there be a sweep-swish-swoon there hiding behind a shivering shadow refined, thus, up…up…goes the lark torpedoing to ascend from its perch the search for cover from pelting raindrops and the sounds of the splosh-pop-plops upon rooftops…

Yet, my mind wonders, assailing not plundered thoughts seeking the beyond yonder!

Yeah, somewhere around the world the pinache…pinache…pinache whispering swiveled-swirled encircled by a quiet crevice, an appealing shadow in peroet silently whistling about me missing you in sweet memory…

**<u>"I REALLY LIKE HOW YOU APPEAL TO ME CAN'T EXPLAIN IT BAAABY…"</u>**

My face skimmed, kissed by crimson, a purple, red-orange tinge prism-in-fade with the crystal drops wetted with the night while my heart palpitates, the eyes glaze-over…

**<u>"RED ROVER…RED ROVER…STROKE THE LOVE IN MY HEART…OVER AND OVER AND SHOULD LAVENDER BE THE COLOR ABOVE HER…LET JASMINE BE WAFTING ALL-AROUND HER…WHILE THE GRINDING STONES OF LIFE PRESENTED 'CINNAMON STRIPED WHITE ROSE IN POSE'…OH</u>**

## STROKE THE FURS OF MY HEARTS WONDER MARINATED TENDER KISS AND BROKE GROUND WITH THUNDER OHH MY SOUL REMINISE!!!"

And in every moment of joy let it reign supreme as the quality time of you and I refined; A togetherness which shreds the pains of my aloneness, and should I heal from the caring look of beauty shining upon your countenance threads of unbroken love mend into our happiness!

Yes, so few people know this, that the power of true "oneness" is worthy of us, and should you ever attempt to let it go, it will recall the life lived in "us-both";

In and out of my existence you go…the thoughts of never letting each other gooo!

## "I REALLY LIKE HOW YOU APPEAL TO ME CAN'T EXPLAIN IT BAAABY…"

And from a kiss…kiss…kiss the climb into my soul to take every morning I wake the sweetness of your breath my nostrils intake, oh, how spectacular is the sight as the 'bright morning star' beams into you from afar, then, the shredded seams of human means begin to dream again mind bends extend…win…win!

Let not this moment pretend since palpable beats of mine own heart born again thumpty-thump brilliantly highlighted never farsighted…

Let not the solace within settle your bones into fragmented tones can we bend the moment to our hearts ascend? Yeah, me all over you and you all over me once again.

## "I REALLY LIKE HOW YOU APPEAL TO ME CAN'T EXPLAIN IT BAAABY…I..I…I"

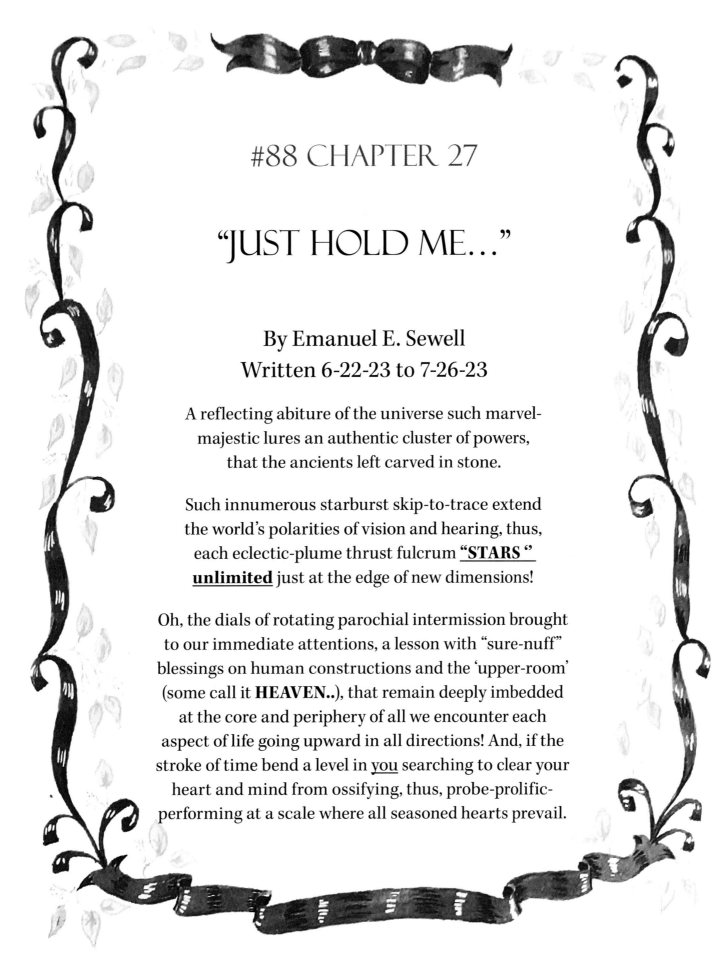

# #88 CHAPTER 27

# "JUST HOLD ME…"

By Emanuel E. Sewell
Written 6-22-23 to 7-26-23

A reflecting abiture of the universe such marvel-majestic lures an authentic cluster of powers, that the ancients left carved in stone.

Such innumerous starburst skip-to-trace extend the world's polarities of vision and hearing, thus, each eclectic-plume thrust fulcrum **"STARS "** **unlimited** just at the edge of new dimensions!

Oh, the dials of rotating parochial intermission brought to our immediate attentions, a lesson with "sure-nuff" blessings on human constructions and the 'upper-room' (some call it **HEAVEN..**), that remain deeply imbedded at the core and periphery of all we encounter each aspect of life going upward in all directions! And, if the stroke of time bend a level in <u>you</u> searching to clear your heart and mind from ossifying, thus, probe-prolific-performing at a scale where all seasoned hearts prevail.

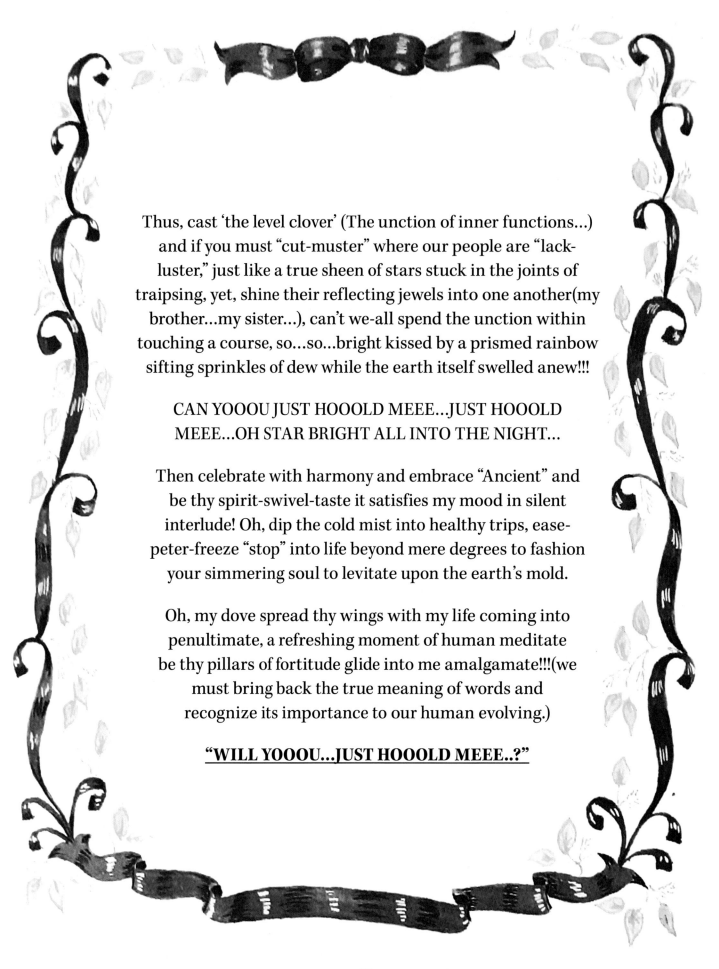

Thus, cast 'the level clover' (The unction of inner functions...) and if you must "cut-muster" where our people are "lack-luster," just like a true sheen of stars stuck in the joints of traipsing, yet, shine their reflecting jewels into one another(my brother...my sister...), can't we-all spend the unction within touching a course, so...so...bright kissed by a prismed rainbow sifting sprinkles of dew while the earth itself swelled anew!!!

CAN YOOOU JUST HOOOLD MEEE...JUST HOOOLD MEEE...OH STAR BRIGHT ALL INTO THE NIGHT...

Then celebrate with harmony and embrace "Ancient" and be thy spirit-swivel-taste it satisfies my mood in silent interlude! Oh, dip the cold mist into healthy trips, ease-peter-freeze "stop" into life beyond mere degrees to fashion your simmering soul to levitate upon the earth's mold.

Oh, my dove spread thy wings with my life coming into penultimate, a refreshing moment of human meditate be thy pillars of fortitude glide into me amalgamate!!!(we must bring back the true meaning of words and recognize its importance to our human evolving.)

**"WILL YOOOU...JUST HOOOLD MEEE..?"**

# #92 CHAPTER 28

# "HERE AND NOW-ONE ON ONE!"

## By Emanuel E. Sewell
## Written 5-2-22 to 8-5-22

<u>Pop quiz:</u> tell me where the heart of the storm is? And the second step is an emersion-mystify-multiply, that which is in the 'mind's eye!'

Cast into the center of the earth where thrashing torrents of the deep annealed blue waters toss and churn by unbreakable cyclones from the storms reverberating lightning bursts,

my pulse skips to clutch where warmed blood trickled through my veins, no time to await we are covered drenched by scudded clouds above us darkening to each thunder-clap!

In this moment the electric-dance was eidetic-in-mind (synaptic-gap...) traversed eclectic-mello-dramatic the deep space static tamped-down on the fiery skyline as the baton was passed the winds eased-up, to remember the demands of invisible commands!

Oh, I get a rush that stills my soul. It's "swish-swash-oshkosh" then I think someday we may even touch from the "dash-flash-poof-blur...winds of the speeds beneath sound, abound!"

Yeah, springtime sprung though cool breezes still stung upon the skin to taste, and switched its gale for heated winds to prevail.

And as I looked on in the distance to land binoculars in both hands leaning on what has yet to come garnishing the storm with a buoyant bounce violet and maroon flailing florals bobbing agility and swaying mobility speaks to natures ambulate no-await, even as lilacs, pansies, black eyed susan's reach for each others petals to shake branches askance patty-caked romanced; And thus, peering down upon what beauty the earth produces even in its dances high-up to the canopy of tree-tops where towering Oaks 'a willow-the-wisp' tip-toeing upon its own display of leafy eye grasp just the right moment in rarity, as if coming alive sparks of polarity, indicating human souls in contemplation (Up...Up...Up... and atoms this ain't no "phantasm-cataclysmic-cycle sheen"); Up with the lone dove spreading in segue its precious wings, and oh, that perked-up watching cannot disguise the fire in my eyes ' you make me feel like I also can "Fly."

### "HERE AND NOW-SUMMER SENSE-ONE ON ONE..."

What I want is too hot for the mind to handle simmering thoughts of its 'summer sense preamble,' just listen, fall back into the liquefied lightning a crisp swishing tipping upon my mid-brain's splash-splosh-slosh of a remiss skipping off major water sources, mystified tender souls sought an embrace with the dawn instead of crimson!

Thus, Sun-beams parched the land again between criss-crossed shadows cut-in-twain easing onward as my palpitating heart-beats 'echoed above the den' from nature's architecture each design seemed to blow the mind!

Pop Quiz what it is? How do you predict the future iridescent so pleasant with a grappling hook heave-hoe posit-pose dowse me again it's the torrential-slip-over me begin, the divine swirl-curl-ripple receive pleas instead of degrees "'all-the-world magnetic-jejune-tingling-tunes-portfolio-dynamite at the height of heights!!!" Thus, nothing oxygen stricken no need to cry billowous intent, yet, it rushed in white plush cottony clouds kissed the azure-skyline in its search to once more splay raindrops upon the earth again for additional rebirth.

Also lifting the haze of particle permissions parlaying adjacent to its heavenly replacement? How astonished and not admonished a tailing rainbow aglow. Yes, a sultant of crystallite gleams peering down spright while on a hilltop the coptering of falling leaves were caressed by autumn's-breeze at the moment of atoning bowing into the earth to create new birth!

### "HERE AND NOW-SUMMER SENSE-ONE ON ONE..."

A spangled-plume stretched fulcrum signaling to the moon if the world had a balance all eyes would gaze at its "insides' ' the meet-up with no plight it's the symmetric-electric-figurine-enigmatic Fantastic! **A Souls' Vision "Climatic."**

### "HERE AND NOW SEEKING 'SEASONS SENSE' HIDDEN IN THE NOOK FROM WHAT THE PANDEMIC TOOK!"

*A tremble and shiver of my life was the height that brought into my mind new insight. And as I walked upon the edge of day yellow-gold in me!*

Printed in the United States
by Baker & Taylor Publisher Services